Niklas Maak
Living Complex

Niklas Maak
Living Complex
From Zombie City to the New Communal

HIRMER

Contents

Chapter 3: Different Houses

Chapter 4: A Short History of the Single-Family Home

Chapter 5: After the House, beyond the Nuclear Family

Chapter 6: Transformations of Privacy

Chapter 7: Shared Spaces

Chapter 8: Closed and Open Systems

Chapter 9: Atmospheres

Chapter 10: Change the Laws!

Christian Wulff in front of his house in Großburgwedel

Problems of
Contemporary Architecture

Holding on to the idyll
The man with the lawn sprinkler

A man stands in a garden, his shirt open, smiling cheerfully into the camera, in front of this brick house with its half-hip roof pulled down over its forehead. Stone edging delineates a square where a neatly trimmed box tree is poised. In his hand the man holds something like a shower head that shoots a stream of water. I am just like you, the photograph communicates, I relax while sprinkling the lawn in my pretty, well-watered garden.

The man presenting himself to the press in the garden of his single-family home near the city of Hanover is Christian Wulff, the former president of the Federal Republic of Germany, and before that, governor of Lower Saxony. Shortly after the pictures of the house circulated, Wulff was no longer in office: on February 17, 2012 he was forced to resign over an affair that began with the desire to have a house in the countryside—and with the problem of coming up with the money for it. In 2008, Wulff had accepted a 500,000 euro loan for the planned house from his friends, the entrepreneur Egon Geerkens and his wife. A few journalists got wind of this and so did the opposition; in response to a parliamentary question in the Landtag (state parliament), Wulff explained that he did not have business relations with Geerkens. He was exposed as a liar and started acting nervous: he left awkward messages on the voice mailboxes of journalists—and shortly thereafter he was forced out of his job. It is a sad story: if Wulff had decided against a half-hip-roof house in the countryside near Hanover in 2008, he would probably still be president today and live in the considerably larger Bellevue Palace in Berlin.

The photograph of the president in front of his overpriced home is a picture of the kind of disaster that repeats itself everywhere: a man standing in front of a house he cannot afford; a man running into debt for the dream of an idyll that plunges him into ruin.

Many of the major crises of today are essentially real estate crises. Almost all have to do with housing: the scandal of Christian Wulff was fundamentally that of someone who absolutely wants a house but does not have the money for it. That also happens to be the story of the housing bubble in the US that triggered the global financial crisis.

Climate change and the social divide are exacerbated by the widespread and persistent desire for a house in the countryside. In parallel, rising housing prices in urban centers force many others outside of the city, where they theoretically have the chance to enjoy a few square feet of lawn. But the ex-urbanite is all too often condemned to a long commute to work in a family car that costs even more money and spoils the very air and tranquility for which they had moved to the countryside in the first place. The result: debt, stress from congested traffic, and growing disillusionment with the countryside, which is no longer the countryside when millions of people move there, but rather, at best, a suburbanized, overcrowded, completely misbuilt, and reduced version of it.

But what is anyone doing about all this? Very little. Suburbanization advances; the "revival of the city centers," much touted by urban marketing, is confined to beautifying gentrified neighborhoods through the addition of cafés and street furniture. Rather than reviving the city for all and establishing and implementing a right for everyone to use the city, developers and planners convert the city center into a luxury playground for a wealthy elite and tourists. These lucky few are presented with a fully functional City Center Theme Park, complete with tons of urban décor.

Why are our cities so desolate, the suburbs a disaster, the houses—with just a few exceptions—so unworthy of discussion and ugly in spite of all the efforts to beautify them?

Housing as fetish

It cannot be said that no one is concerned with the issue of housing. On the contrary: housing is a subject addressed everywhere. Home-related TV shows abound; wherever you go, there seems to be constant chatter about apartments, residences, rising rents, furnishings. Dwelling has developed into an all-determining fetish—from a necessity into the ultimate *raison d'être*: people work so as to live in a beautiful place. They buy kitchens for the price of mid-size cars, so as to spend time with friends and family there. But because they have to work so much for the property and its innards, there is almost no time left to actually *live* there. Housing has become the main objective of all of life's endeavors: at many newsstands, the widest shelf is the one with home magazines. Nowhere is the fetishization of housing more obvious then here. In the 1960s and 1970s those magazines still looked like sales catalogs for spaceships and they hailed, with extraterrestrial euphoria, new houses as the dawning of a more beautiful and more exciting modern world. Today the thrust is different: it is no longer about new departures, but rather about comforting self-immersion. When opening one of the magazines, you see satin-smooth pillows, sofas as soft as swamps, beds awash in down covers, flowing curtains that are thick as walls and behind which the drab outside world disappears—and any sense of the causes of its misery along with it. The goal of all home-décor-magazine dreams is not a buoyant, wild life, but rather relaxation, sleep, and isolation. The single-family home becomes, once and for all, a temple of immersion: despite huge kitchen tables which obstruct space like monuments of an unfulfilled desire, it is no longer about inviting guests and partying together, but about sleeping undisturbed among dangling tassels. Try to find pictures showing fifteen people partying at a ravaged table, on sofas and in kitchens in any of the home décor magazines.

The home furnishings and decorative ideas testify to the occupant's sense of being overwhelmed by life. The house is a wellness landscape for the overworked and burnout-stricken homeowner, a comfort zone where everything is geared to rest, seclusion, comfort and that at the same time makes the owner forget that the house, the stress, and the costs it incurs are themselves one of the primary reasons for his or her exhaustion.

Why do millions of people behave as if it were an anthropological necessity to get up to their ears in debt in order to move into a house that has to have at least 1,600 square feet, a basement, a double carport, and a toolshed?

The facile answer is, because in one's own home—unlike at the office, where one earns a wage in a state of alienation and subjugation, in public space and other areas of life—one can be one's own master; because one becomes economically emancipated from issues such as retirement planning and rent increases; because one believes that the money is safely invested in something of lasting value—though considering the quality of today's new construction, one might quite sensibly ask whether a house will outlive a car.

Construction has become too expensive. A good many building owners can no longer afford walls the way they still used to be built as recently as the 1960s. Nor, however, can they afford the façade that is quickly put up with hastily added insulation and applied plaster: it may last ten years, perhaps, until massive damage appears. Anyone building a fully thermally insulated house today can already brace him or herself for having to renew the façade every ten years—which is a long-term bonanza for the insulation industry: every job automatically returns every ten years.

Empty shells for lifestyles that no longer exist

But there seem to be few convincing alternatives to the single-family house. When it comes to the proper architectural setting for private life that can also serve as insurance against old-age poverty or inflation, the options have thus far been depressingly scant. For most people, the answer is buying a small or large apartment or a small or large house, as finances allow.

What results is a lifestyle imposed by an architectural form, rather than the other way around: Father, mother, child, pet, and the van in the carport. The architectural forms we take for granted cannot even answer the simple question of how people should live with dependent (grand)parents, or with partners with children. Housing as we know it is so geared to a certain norm that these arrangements only exist as emergencies. The standardization of lifestyles has its equivalent in the standardization of the public spaces that surround residential buildings: if people meet each other at all, it is as spectators at events or in public spaces shaped by commerce where social rituals are predetermined by consumption activities: just to be allowed to be there, one has to order drinks or food, buy a movie ticket, or at least pretend to be interested in buying something while strolling through stores.

And so a basic problem with urban planning and building policy begins with this misconception of what people want to do in a public square or inside an apartment. State housing associations, real estate developers, and builders ask all too seldom for whom they are really building. They ignore the fact that Western societies are aging rapidly, resulting in a population that no longer has the same spatial and financial resources as previous generations and must live at a reduced scale simply because of economic constraints. And they ignore another important demographic trend: society is heading toward the point where the classic family no longer represents the majority. In other words, they are building for a lifestyle that no longer exists as such.

The basic types of architecture that dominate in our part of the world today—apartment and house—were mostly geared to a lifestyle that saw individuals follow a clear pattern. In this model, after a brief phase as singles living in efficiencies or studio apartments while studying or going through training, high-skilled workers and professionals found a classic nuclear family which subsequently moves to a house in the countryside or a three-bedroom apartment in the city. According to an analysis by the German Federal Institute of Demography, Germany is among the countries with the highest percentage of single-person households, about 40 percent, of all countries in Europe—only Norway and Denmark ranked higher. In the major cities the number was even over 50 percent in 2011; in Berlin and Munich, families are by now almost a marginal group—their share of all households no more than between 14 and 20 percent.

How do politicians, planners, architects, and builders respond to this fundamental change? Everyone thinks they know what functions a unit should incorporate. But what exists, what happens exactly inside and in front of a unit? How do the shifts in social rituals, demographic change, the technological transformation of jobs, the dissolution of the classic office, and the break-up of the classic nuclear family affect building? Building is tailored to two forms of existence: singles or families. But this is a normative sociopolitical construct. We do not know of a convincing type of building that would be suitable for six octogenarians who are otherwise unwilling to move into a retirement home. We do not know of a type of building where three single parents could live with their children and two gay friends, unless they had enough money to rent a mansion and install additional bathrooms there. Nor do we know of a convincing new type of building where people live for a longer period of time and where they can also accommodate refugees or transients more easily than would otherwise be possible. Building policies also shape society by discouraging such lifestyles. Good architecture, however, is always an encouragement to try out new ways of life. What forms might a public square, a house, an apartment take, beyond those we are familiar with? Is it conceivable that there are forms that enable more freedom, because they create less economic pressure? If rents or mortgage payments were halved from what people pay today, most people would be able to work less—and would have more time for what, aside from watching TV and going to sleep, is called living.

The problem of structure and form
The cult of downsizing

Many planners believe they can escape demographic pressures by simply scaling down familiar types of housing. In 2012, at the urging of Mayor Michael Bloomberg, the City of New York sponsored a design competition for small apartments, or "micro-units," because by then a third of the city's population was composed of "singles." The proposal was to reduce the minimum legal unit size from the current 400 to 275 square feet—a move that pleases the building industry more than it troubles it, because if the space thus saved is not used for collective zones or for communal gardens and kitchens, it just means that the building industry gets to squeeze more apartments into the same space as before. Rather than encouraging new forms of housing and lifestyles and a more responsible use of resources, this apparent response to demographic change merely serves as an excuse for another market-friendly radical economization of housing. With a few exceptions, the results of the New York competition are reminiscent of what American car manufacturers did in the 1970s in response to the oil shock: they simply downsized an existing, dysfunctional large object. A huge limousine was shrunk to create a ridiculously downscaled limousine with a tiny interior, and the resulting car still managed to get poor gas mileage; similarly, already cramped apartments become even more cramped. Underlying this is the misconception that in order to save energy and money, one can simply downsize a form, rather than structurally reimagine it.

At the same time, a zoning mandate stays untouched that requires private developers to build parking spaces for new apartments in certain parts of the city. As Michael Kimmelman, the architecture critic for *The New York Times*, writes, "it forces developers to spend what a study by the Furman Center at New York University estimates is up to $50,000 per parking space, money inevitably charged to consumers, increasing housing costs. [...] If you add up all the street-level parking spaces on housing authority lots around town, you get more than 20.3 million square feet, well over half the size of Central Park."[1]

Many forms—houses as well as public squares—rely on the easy fix of formally referencing something that used to work well, instead of researching the structural conditions that made it work.

What exactly is a public square today, now that the need for urban squares as marketplaces or for courtly representation no longer exists?

Without answering this question, without taking a step back from the concept and its potential meaning, people will be unable to build really novel squares and will, instead, just keep senselessly repeating ever fainter visions of the classic Italian piazza, although none of the conditions that once determined the form of those squares exists anymore. The rebuilt piazza is invariably a memory of something that no longer exists, the expression of a longing that is confused with its fulfillment.

Although lifestyles, social rituals, economic conditions, concepts of family, life plans, and housing desires are changing, the meager selection of architectural shells remains the same.

A billion housing units

Yet the housing issue also arises on a different, more existential level. In New York, as of this writing, 22,000 children live on the street, the highest number since the Depression of 1929.[2] In Sub-Saharan Africa, 72 percent of the population lives in slums; in Southeast Asia, the number is 59 percent.[3] The United Nations expects world population to increase by at least 1.5 billion people by 2050, and by as much as 2.5 billion according to its intermediate scenario. "In Asia alone the number of households may reach 1.5 billion by 2030," writes Tobias Just, head of sector and real estate market analysis at Deutsche Bank Research. "That is 75 percent higher than at the turn of the millennium. The dynamics are similarly strong in Latin America, a little less so in North America, and even stronger still in Africa. Even in Europe the increase is quite substantial at about 16 percent." In the coming two decades "more than 700 million households will be added. But because urbanization is advancing rapidly especially in Africa and Asia and the relocation of a household from the countryside to the city creates an additional need for housing, about a billion more dwellings need to be completed by 2030 to meet demand."[4]

Even if this number seems very high, analysts agree that hundreds of millions of new dwellings will need to be built. The question that concerns us now is: what form will these dwellings take?

Most of their occupants will not have the money to finance a house as we know it, or even an apartment in a high-rise. Because of the service and operating costs—for elevators, for instance—and the high construction costs, high-rises in Asia and Latin America are now already forms of housing for the middle class. According to UN Habitat, 400 million city dwellers already live in critically overcrowded accommodations, especially in South Asia and India, where over a third of the urban population lives in spaces occupied by more than three people. Both economically and ecologically, it will be impossible to meet the housing demand with traditional architectural and urbanistic methods and forms.

What form will new houses and apartments in built-up areas take? The problem is exacerbated by the adoption of Western forms of urban sprawl in Asia. Traffic jams in the major Chinese cities have taken on apocalyptic dimensions, even though the population concentration in the large cities of China and India is still relatively low according to statistics compiled by the German Federal Agency for Civic Education:[5] only three percent of the urban population of

China live in Shanghai, whereas 42 percent of the Japanese urban population live in the metropolitan area of Tokyo (according to the 2005 census, about 35.7 million people, with a population density of 13,415 people per square kilometer). It is not difficult to imagine what will happen if the Chinese metropolises catch up with Japan in terms of traffic and population density. If only because of dwindling resources, the European and American model of the suburb has come to its end: millions of new city dwellers will no longer be able to live in the endlessly sprawling bungalow developments from where they commute to work in their midsize sedans. How else should they live, though? Optimists hope that the shrinking cities of the East European and American provinces will flourish again as a result of new attractive industries, location-independent computer jobs, and a growing sense of suburban fatigue. But in Asia, Africa, and Latin America, the issue is how to provide residents, within the smallest area and for as little money possible, with spaces for privacy as well as communal spaces that transcend familiar building typologies—and how to cleverly convert and repopulate buildings (estates, factory halls, administration buildings) that have been abandoned in huge numbers in the thinned-out peripheries and areas beset by population loss in Europe and North America.

The two crises of housing

There are two crises of housing. In one case it is about pure survival and in the other about what society we want to live in and what this society prioritizes: in what spaces people want to meet, where they want to be private and where sociable, how it defines privacy and publicness in general, and what form new spaces for this could take. The question of how the—ecologically and economically no longer sustainable—suburban housing sprawl and urban desolation in the industrial nations can be contained is fundamentally different from the question of how to accommodate migrant workers in India, Asia, and Africa in the first place and to provide a minimum degree of protection and meeting places for social activities. The two questions need to be addressed with very different architectural, urbanistic, and political means. But then again these distinct problem areas have a lot in common, including the lack of ideas for fundamentally new, inexpensive dwellings that could conform to changed social conditions or encourage such change. In both cases new building typologies need to be developed. In both cases there is a need to reflect on what "housing," "being private," and "public space" means; what a dwelling is supposed to protect against and how; and how much place a person really needs. Many people consider 1,400 square feet with basement the absolute minimum space for a family of four and get into debt for "appropriately" sized houses: but this is because there are so few convincing counterexamples.

Why is it that the major architecture firms in particular have devoted relatively little effort to new forms of low-income housing since the 1970s? The answer is simple: a lack of commissions. The state has abandoned large-scale housing projects, and affordable housing has not been attractive for private investors due to meager profit expectations. Moreover, "housing" is considered the antithesis to "architecture," or, as Susanne Schindler, one of the leading housing researchers, once put it: "'Housing' is that quantitative, socioeconomic beast, to be produced at lowest possible cost, while 'architecture' is seen, most definitely since the mid-1970s, as a cultural endeavor, reserved for museums and high-rises and quite possibly 'houses,' but most definitely not 'housing.'"[6]

Super objects
The pitfalls of Parametricism

In the media the prevailing image of architecture is as an art of creating the most spectacular sculptural supersigns for deep-pocketed public or private clients—even though most people are likely to spend a mere thousandth of their time in front of those supersigns, while the rest of their lives passes by in suburbs, administrative buildings, and other agglomerations of buildings that no one, with the exception of a few trade journalists, feels like talking about, not least because they look so drab.

Part of contemporary architecture, moreover, is stuck in Parametricism, the application of parametric design systems and digital animation and scripting techniques to architecture. Parametricism essentially only means designing a digital model on the computer with the aid of parameters. Each parameter can be changed, resulting in complex geometries, and in the end one form out of thousands can be selected, which is then built. It is important to distinguish between parametricism as an analysis tool for complex phenomena such as pedestrian flows, which can be better controlled thanks to parametric analyses, and Parametricism as an architectural style. In simple terms: you can analyze complex urban processes with complex mathematical formulas and you can describe urban compaction as the forming of a swarm made up of many individual structures.

In response to this you can build houses that are very plain or houses that look like extraterrestrial insects. The latter is Parametricism as a style: its structures look like three-dimensional statistic curves or bionic monsters, or as if modern classics had been rebuilt in sliced cheese and then microwaved. This soft-cheese architecture is easy to design and extremely difficult to build, and ultimately it almost always results in completely dysfunctional buildings that seem to renounce their status as buildings per se. They seem to want to function as artworks that, ultimately, and under great sacrifices, may be habitable. They serve the market of super-signs with which solvent clients create a monument to their prosperity and dynamism. Ultimately, Parametricism as a style is elaborate kitsch: the Sacré Cœur of the digital age.

How to argue about architecture?

People argue far too little, on the other hand, about the architecturally scantily defined suburbs, city districts, and towns where daily life takes place between supermarkets, playgrounds, gas stations, office districts, and home improvement stores—which is why it is not surprising that nostalgia and isolation are by now the prevailing strategies when it comes to housing and that the past decade has been characterized by a collective escape into home improvement, giving rise—with all the TV shows, home décor magazines, and discount furniture retailers—to a consciousness industry whose ideal customer is the immobilized citizen on the sofa.

At the same time, the things happening in cities no longer have anything to do with a normal process of gentrification where a more affluent middle class drives off low-income people to other neighborhoods. By now, lawyers and doctors can just as little afford certain locations in urban centers as families, retirees, storekeepers, students, workers, café owners, and small entrepreneurs. All those who once made up an urban culture—understood as the concentration, overlapping, intermixture, and mutual enrichment of different population strata—are being pushed out to make space for offices, hotels, shopping malls, facilities for the general entertainment of tourists, and a few luxury residential properties that are often acquired as capital investment and sit empty most of the time. The city center is changing from a space to live into a walkable investment portfolio, with a few delicatessen shops and other special product stores keeping the most essential things on hand, just in case a condominium owner does happen to drop by.

How do we want to live, in what kind of cities, what kind of dwellings? This question is old and important—and flawed. For who is the "we"? Everyone dwells and everyone has a different idea of what life should be like. For this reason alone it is not easy to argue about architecture. For whenever a person who comes along and says: "Your cities are a disaster! Your houses are wretched scaled-down versions of the notion of a house and your squares forbidding," another person comes along and says: "That may be your opinion: we think it is beautiful." For every aesthetically sensitive lover of the classic European city who inveighs against big-box architecture with its lack of proportion, another person will defend those boxes as part of a modern urban aesthetic—and in this way the debate sinks into the quagmire of judgments of taste that elude generalization. And then there is the question how social, technological, and demographic change affects habitation. We are told over and over again that there is no need to call the entire house into question just because the music now comes from an iPod and the laptop makes it possible to work from home: people still have to sleep and want to feel secure and not get wet when it rains outside. These, too, are among the arguments that play into the hands of the building industry, which is only moderately interested in changes: namely, the claim that "dwelling" and the associated needs are basic anthropological constants—and that there is no need to change anything about the house, just because the social rituals taking place inside and in front of it have changed.

The anthropologization of habitation

Time and again attempts to find a way out of this quagmire have reverted to anthropological arguments. In an essay titled "Gib mir Simse: Was ist zeitgemäßes Bauen" (Gimme Ledges: What Is Contemporary Architecture), the German architect Hans Kollhoff attempted a radical redefinition by almost going back to the primates and claiming that there is an "anthropomorphous constant of the architectural," timelessly readable "architectonics" that establish an "unconscious communication between man and his artifacts."[7] In this way a biologistical basis is provided for good architecture: "man in general" simply wants pointed roofs and a "pitched roof with gable" has "a physiognomic advantage over a flat roof"—statements that are about as meaningful as claiming that a hatted head has a physiognomic advantage over a head with side parting. The still popular notion that the flat roof is the result of rationalist Modernism and that for formal, ideological reasons it has, like a breakfast egg, decapitated the traditional pointed-roof house—as the form appropriate to man—is known to be wrong: as early as about 3000 BC, Herodotus reports, bitumen was used for flat roofs; in the Hanging Gardens of Semiramis the waterproofing consisted of asphalt tiles, bricks, and mortar; and as early as the Baroque period, architects such as Jakob Marperger advocated green roof surfaces. The anthropologizing archaizers do not care about any of this. With reference to alleged anthropological constants, Gert Selle, in his "hidden history of habitation," similarly explains that "aspirations are too regressive, memories too binding for habitation ... to become subject to revolutionary change."[8] Dwelling has "remained an anthropological constant, part of the balance of needs, whose origins lie in the murky process of man's humanization." People are like "nest-building creatures that are genetically programmed to know what curvature of a depression is just right for the brooding

22

and the brood." A chapter of Selle's book is devoted to "Archetypes of Space,"[9] "ancient images going back to the obscure early history of cultural experience," and he lists among those images the pointed roof, which is still found today in every children's drawing as a shorthand symbol for "house." Once plunged as "ancient" into the murkiness of the "process of man's humanization," claims such as these defy any further verifiability: could it be that children have simply seen an endless number of houses with pointed roofs in children's books, Playmobil cities, and drawings of their kindergarten teachers by the time they are able to draw a house with a pointed roof—in other words, that this cipher is not innate, but rather learned like the first letter of one's own name? What happens when one asks a child living in a Bauhaus residence to paint a house? The child paints what it knows: a house with a flat roof. Well then? Even neuroscience has recently discovered architecture as a subject of research, focusing on the possible existence of supraindividual, objectifiable dwelling needs and particularly suitable architectural forms related to those needs. The fact that there are individual historical experiences which change ideas about housing is no longer a primary concern here. By contrast, the sociologists Hartmut Häußermann and Walter Siebel write in their *Soziologie des Wohnens*: "Taking ahistorical conditions ('How does man dwell?') as the starting point in analyzing habitation proves to be absurd. […] If you abstract from forms of habitation that are specific for particular periods, cultures, and social classes, the only common denominator remaining is the physical protective function of housing. And that, in fact, does not distinguish human dwellings from the fox's burrow or the beehive. What actually does distinguish man from animal is, as Karl Marx has convincingly explained, man's ability to design and construct his own world."[10]

No one wants to freeze to death or be assaulted—humans, cats, and reptiles agree on this. Any other basic anthropological constants for habitation, however, are difficult to find. But how was it possible then for, say, the single-family house to become an apparent natural constant in the architecture of cities and suburbs?

The reasons why the single-family house has managed to prevail as a form of housing and to still be dominant today are mainly economic. This is often forgotten in the debate that even neuroscience contributes to nowadays. Along with the big and long apartment blocks of urban housing developments, the single-family house is the form of habitation with which the building industry, meaning general contractors, solid-house contractors, craftsmen, and manufacturers of construction materials, can make the highest profits. This clear economic motivation creates pressure to increase standardization processes in the building trade, which eventually results in the same old, drab forms of housing. It is part of the game to obscure this economic motivation—the consequences of which the occupants get to bear—to tout the single-family house as an anthropological necessity and thereby raise it to the status of an indisputable natural form of existence to which there is no alternative.

Many respond to the consequences of this aggressive lobbying by the building industry with depressive cynicism, saying that architecture is just a reflection of the societal power constellations and that every society gets the architecture it deserves.

One could also ask the question the other way around, of course: what power structures, lobbies, and interest groups prevent a society from building the spaces it would like to have?

Revolt against the building mafia
In defense of habitology

No one builds a house for him or herself: anyone who wants to know why houses look the way they do and why there do not seem to be any alternatives must ask about the political entities that are responsible for building permits and codes and about the interests of the agents of the building trade, meaning the investors, building contractors, and, intricately intertwined, the industry, which has its own commercial agenda. A precise political science of habitation that does not engage in hazy psychological and anthropological speculation should first sort out the power structures that shape habitation and its current forms: who has an interest in houses and cities looking the way they do? Without this economic materialistic approach, speaking about architecture remains a matter of taste-based aesthetic judgments and unsophisticated cultural pessimism that ascribes the ugliness of the suburbs solely to a lack of civic common sense and education in good taste. Such a debate about urban culture fails to acknowledge the real commercial interests that shape it. What is touted as the "return of a civic living culture" to the city center, for instance, often consists essentially of expensive housing monocultures that, if anything, are characterized by the displacement of everything constituting civic urban culture—if this is understood to mean the mixing, compacting, amalgamating, conflating of heterogeneous influences into a community.

Instead of the endless formal-ideological, metaphysical debate about the appropriate form of housing for "mankind in general," it would be much more interesting to just accept that there are both good houses with flat roofs and good houses with pointed roofs, both good houses made of glass and good houses made of stone, both good perimeter development and good cityscapes and people who more or less like each of those—and instead to ask about structural economic conditions: what lobbies and power interests are reflected in the architectural forms? Why is it that so many new urban neighborhoods are developed that no one wants to be subsequently responsible for and that, beyond all differences in taste, no one really likes? Why do we not hear anything about the lobbies that architecturally lay waste to the country? Because the radical economization of building is complemented by a depoliticization of the discourse on building. Outside of universities and symposia there is no broad-based discussion about the question of what the public places in which we want to meet one another should be like, what our cities and houses should offer—and who prevents these houses and cities from being built.

Perhaps is not even due to the questionable taste of the occupants that residential neighborhoods outside of the city look so drab, but rather to the lack of alternatives: the industry of the turnkey-ready confines individual decisions to door décors and dormer forms; anything else would run counter to the dictate of maximum profitability. A new habitology would have to be a critical science, a political economy of architecture which traces the power and interest structures that are reflected in—or hide behind—new construction and urbanistic master plans; for building is, in the vast majority of cases, not primarily an aesthetic but more an economic discipline which, unfortunately, also clearly shows in most buildings.

That no alternatives to the familiar forms are offered in, say, the field of housing construction is also due to the interests of a building industry that makes good money with cheaply built single-family cubes in the countryside and depressing apartment blocks in the city and which dreads nothing as much as the question: How else could we dwell?

In order to understand what could come after the house as we know it, one should be familiar with the history of the single-family house—and that of the alternatives that have always existed. In terms of cultural history, the single-family house with a pointed gable roof that is occupied by the nuclear family and so eagerly propagandized by the building industry is, in fact, a quite recent invention and a result of nineteenth-century industrialization. For millennia, building complexes were the rule and significantly more than four related people, on average, lived in them together, whether they were farmsteads or palaces or bourgeois townhouses. What seems like an experimental residential commune to us today was for centuries the norm.

Even notions of what being "private" means has changed radically over the course of the history of building. The history of the bedroom, the living room, the kitchen, or the children's room reveals that dwelling is not a static affair. It shows that spaces, furnishings, forms of housing can be rethought. And it also shows that there were frequent attempts to make housing easier, less expensive, to reduce it to its essence, in order to achieve greater independence from lease costs and furniture loans.

Radicalized spatial qualities

According to a study of the German Federal Institute of Demography, living-space consumption per capita increased from 420 to 485 square feet just in the fifteen-year period from 1998 to 2013; in 1950 it was at 160 square feet. In the states of the former West Germany a total living space of 31.2 billion square feet was occupied in 2005; since 1993 this space has increased by more than four billion square feet. Since 1993, demand for living space in the new eastern states has increased by 1.16 billion square feet and living-space consumption per household is up by 74 percent.[11] This has an impact on the landscape. In Germany, between 245 and 300 acres are converted for habitation and traffic purposes on a daily basis. This expansion has ecological and economic implications, of course.

Especially in America, a process of rethinking is setting in with the small house and tiny house movements. A tiny house has a maximum of about 600 square feet of living space and a small house a maximum of about 1,200 square feet, which in the 1950s was still considered a normal size for a house, but today can only be regarded as small when taking into account that the average living space of single-family homes in the US increased from 1,775 square feet in 1978 to 2,475 square feet in 2007.[12] The small house movement shows, among other things, how buildings with solar panels, rainwater catchment systems, and composting toilets can become self-sustaining and look like alternatives to the current insulation using foam blocks—that is, by using natural materials that are much less demanding on resources in their fabrication and use, such as wood, straw, cork, and loam.[13] According to an analysis by the German Passive House Institute,[14] the manufacturing energy that is saved per square foot in building a tiny house can heat the tiny house for a whole year, which means that the energy needed to build a conventional 1,075-square-foot single-family house could be used to heat a tiny house for a hundred years.

Yet curbing the consumption of space is seen as an unreasonable demand. A square-footage fetishism rules when it comes to housing; sharing 800 square feet of living space in a more or less relaxed manner with four people is considered impossible. Yet houses exist that show this is very well possible, if private spaces are radicalized and the resources that are thus opened up and the money and space saved are used for all the more spacious communal areas, such as roof terraces or large collective gardens for ten dwelling units. Privacy in these spaces is not limited, just organized differently. The decrease in living space is a gain rather than a loss: life in a house where everything is reduced to the essentials is so much cozier and more intimate inside and so much more open and spacious on the outside.

There is too much dull space, and there are too many houses where all the rooms look similarly bland. There are too few buildings that save space and costs by radicalizing living atmospheres: making a bedroom so small that it feels cozier than the usual space where the bulky wardrobe stands reproachfully across from the bed and that feels neither especially snug nor particularly open.

Hegemonietempel, Berlin
(House Borries/Tollmann,
architect: Christof Mayer)

There are examples of architecture that saves costs by radicalizing spatial impact. Lacaton & Vassal architects built a very cheap house for a postal employee in Floriac near Bordeaux that really consists of two houses: a small one with tight and cozy spaces and a larger one that is superimposed on the small one like a greenhouse.

During winter the occupants retreat into the snugness of the small house, which is easy to heat, and during summer they have an enormous living room with huge ceiling heights. The situation is similar with the rooftop structure the composer Christian von Borries and curator Vera Tollmann had designed for themselves in Berlin. All that needs to be heated are the two walled dwelling cells where the occupants sleep and live during winter; in between, a simple greenhouse structure creates a huge two-floor living room. The house cost just a third of a cheap single-family house and offers much more spatial variety than a classic old residential building. It is a house where the spaces were radicalized: the bedroom is decidedly private, while the living space is all the more open and airy. The bedroom becomes a cave and the living room a lightly roofed landscape. Habitology, a science of habitation, would have to study such spatial impact and reflect on the question of how various possible dwelling needs—protection and privacy, as well as openness toward the outside world—can be met in formally more purposeful ways, even though the building industry, and especially outdated dogmatic legislation, make every effort to prevent such experiments.

Building law as a problem
Policy demands

In addition to the economic interests of a building industry that is only moderately interested in new forms, there are political and legislative issues that stand in the way of novel residential architecture. In the US, this has given rise to the "making room" movement, an initiative launched in 2009 by the nonprofit advocacy group Citizens Housing and Planning Council (CHPC) with the goal of reforming the regulations that govern the production of housing in New York City. As Susanne Schindler of CHPC explains: "CHPC's analysis shows that regulatory constraints prevent housing that would respond to current demographic developments—more single households, both of elderly but also the young professionals, but also more extended households, either of multiple generations or alternate forms of cohabitation—from being built. For instance, the 'family'—defined as no more than three unrelated adults in one household—is still on the books as the only legal social entity to occupy a dwelling unit. Clearly, no one has the time to enforce these laws, and yet they impact what is funded and approved. Much of CHPC's argument is based on recognizing how people already live; and that the instrument of the market currently cannot respond to these needs."[15]

Can market interests and efforts to preserve the social city even be reconciled? They can—through simple changes to building regulations. One of the simplest proposals of this kind in Germany is to increase the maximum eaves height, which in Berlin is currently at 72 to 85 feet. This would allow for the construction of luxury penthouses—with the condition that owners, in turn, have to commit to renting one floor at 0.6 euro per square foot. This would allow private homeowners and developers of new buildings to construct attractive penthouse apartments that can be rented at high prices, while also enabling thousands of affordable apartments to be instantly created through a single legal decision. That such a win-win situation—which urban thinkers and architects such as Arno Brandlhuber have been calling for again and again—would quasi-automatically result in the desired social mix is just one positive effect.

Housing shortage, vacant housing, and increasing per capita demand are strangely interrelated not least because of misguided building policies: many older people cannot leave their four-bedroom apartments, which are far too large for them, even if they would like to, because they still have an old lease agreement and a new, one-bedroom apartment would be more expensive for them than the largely vacant old one. This, too, is something that new building policies could regulate through subsidies or attractive, low-priced buildings adapted to the needs of elderly people.

Furthermore, in contrast to monotonous bedroom communities, it is not that easy to build a mix of dwelling units, kindergartens, common roof terraces and gardens, perhaps along with a soccer field or a basketball court and small businesses such as bakeries or carpentries where, like in old neighborhoods, one can quickly get a loaf of bread or bring things to be repaired. Current European law regarding building is essentially still informed by the ideals of the Athens Charter and the modern functional division of the city into bedroom communities on the one hand and purely working environments on the other. The fact that concentrations and functional overlaps, the jumble of flower shops, cafés, workshops, and apartments that makes up the appeal of southern European cities, only become possible through exception permits is due mainly to public building law—for instance, to the principle of separation, the German "Act on the Prevention of Harmful Effects on the Environment caused by Air Pollution, Noise, Vibration, and Similar Phenomena"—in short: the Federal Immission Control Act. Issued in 1974, this act was influenced by the American Clean Air Act, which was intended to protect residential neighborhoods from noise and air pollution by nearby business and industrial establishments, yet more often than not resulted in dismally quiet bedroom blocks and single-family housing subdivisions in development areas that would benefit from a bit of carpentry noise, smells of fresh bread baking, and general urban vibration.

The language crisis of architecture

Architects and urban planners complain: on the one hand about the state of their profession, the ignorance of clients, the pressure from general contractors, the greed of real estate developers, and often quite rightly so. Because, on the other hand, times are exciting and good for architects, urbanists, and policy makers in the field, if only because a striking number of the major contemporary crises that need to be solved are essentially real estate crises.

What is needed in order to be able to solve them is not, however, just a close look at the forms, mechanisms, and power structures that shape our lives in houses, on squares, and in the cities, but also a closer look at the language used in architecture to describe, as well as to design and to think.

The architectural world has a language problem. For example, there is the comically garbled language of architectural design competitions, which, incredibly, manages to sound both florid and technocratic ("The building complex fits sensitively into the urban context of the existing fabric and impresses with the stringent opening of the lobby toward public space and the facilitation of community-building experiences"). Then there are the strangely depressive terms used to tout ecologically exemplary houses, such as "passive house" or "zero-energy house"—which sounds like a bad joke: "What is going on with your house; why does it look so sad the way it stands there on the field?—Oh, I don't really know; I guess it's because it's a passive house."

Who wants to live in a "zero-energy house"? The name suggests demure austerity, scratchy wool socks, and cold coffee—and with this a fundamental problem of sustainable products passes over into the building trade: that those products are, of course, ecologically commendable but at the same time also sustainably joyless. For a long time the lack of success of eco-friendly cars and eco-friendly houses was likewise due to the fact that they looked like Protestant-austere self-chastisement products, that they did not propagate a sensual minimalism, a liberating focus on essentials, an ecological futurism, but rather "deceleration" and "stasis." The admonishingly wagging finger was always sticking out of their windows. A grimly ascetic air of anything-prettier-is-not-something-we-can-afford-anymore-today envelops the "passive house" in particular—a residential building that is in any case often faulty reasoning turned to stone, because in order to meet climate protection targets, for which the thermal insulation of the passive house is allegedly indispensable, it may be better to think about what would be really ecological: highly compacted, smart urban architecture which obviates the need to commute to the suburbs, rather than a fully insulated zero-energy subdivision loosely tossed into the landscape.

But there is another, more profound language problem in architecture: the odd vagueness of the concepts with which many architects and planners operate. Twenty years ago one needed an office with a table, a chair, telephone, computer, fax, and printer to work. Now one could hypothetically do all that with just a laptop and a cell phone, while lying in the artificial dunescape of the Rolex Center that SANAA architects from Japan built in Lausanne. Still, most planners think they know what a "public place" and a "workplace" are. Beyond professional circles there is no fundamental, systematic discourse about what "dwelling," "working," and "publicness" could mean in light of changed collective social rituals, technological innovations, and ecological challenges—about what other forms a "house" and a "square," as a private place to retreat to and as a place of "being public," could take in view of changing lifestyles, social rituals, and technical possibilities.

The frequency with which Facebook, NSA, and big data are referred to as threats to privacy is inversely proportional to the astonishing fuzziness of the definition of how "private" and "public" really are to be understood in architecture. When a person has been lying on a bed for eight hours, writing and sending emails, making business calls, buying or selling things on the Internet, skyping, and posting things, and then puts aside cell phone and iPad and goes out into an empty nighttime street for a stroll—what is that person doing? Is that person moving from a private space into a public one? Or is he or she looking for an intimate, private moment of reflection outside after spending the day doing—with the aid of various technological media—what in antiquity took place in so-called public space: exchange of information, trade, debate? This is yet another reason why the discussion of architecture needs a revision of its axioms.

After the house
Rethinking architecture

In many areas of life a new mainstream culture of sharing is emerging. Instead of buying a car, city dwellers join a car-sharing organization; they now only ever borrow garden tools and power drills and rent out their own things. What does this new culture of sharing mean for housing? Could people also share spaces with others, and if so, how? What would remain in terms of a sphere of privacy?

What does it mean for a new kind of collective dwelling beyond the familiar forms of "apartment" and "house" if we assume, as case law does, that dwelling and the identity of a person should be thought of as inextricably linked? What factors beyond categorical distinctions between privacy and publicness ensure that someone feels "chez soi," at home; what role do the atmospheres of places play and what defines such atmospheres?

House NA, Tokyo
(Sou Fujimoto)

Architects such as Ryue Nishizawa, Michael Maltzan, Sou Fujimoto, and Riken Yamamoto have designed collective residential complexes—to which this book devotes a separate chapter, because, unlike in classic residential communities, the occupants of those complexes are not squeezed together into common spaces, come what may. Instead, they live in an assembly of autonomous cells where the private and the collective interpenetrate, complement, and reinforce one another in new ways.

Those buildings are also examples of how architecture can be rethought beyond established concepts and notions. Everyone believes they know what a four-story house should look like. Ninety-nine percent of all architects, when commissioned to build a "four-story house," will stack four approximately 10-foot-high boxes on top of one another and connect them through staircases. More often than not the propositional speech act "four stories" just means that a house should not exceed a height of about 60 feet. What happens when an architect takes the concept of "story" apart is demonstrated by Sou Fujimoto's House NA in Tokyo: instead of four approximately equal-size stories, this house has more than twenty levels connected through small two- to three-step stairs on which the residents' domestic life is organized very differently.

In this case, work on the concept preceded work on the form; the creative freedom lay in being able to subvert and reconceive an unquestioned category that was considered axiomatic.

The aim of this book is to discuss the new residential models and lifestyles that are emerging as a response to the crisis of housing. Are

Microhouse (Liu Lubin)

the dwellings of umpteen millions of workers and low-income earners who are moving into the agglomerations of Asia, Africa, and Latin America to look like what the Chinese architect Liu Lubin has designed: a dwelling cell that is part architecture, part furniture and configured in such a way that one can sit, sleep, or prepare a meal in it? Lubin's minimal cell continues the tradition of radical tiny-house designs and Metabolist urban planning. The three modules of this house contain a bedroom, a bathroom, and a small office: units can be grouped together to make larger dwellings, or neighborhoods. The modules are designed to fit into shipping containers and can be transported easily. As Lubin explains, their size also allows them to bypass current restrictions governing private homes in China.

Would it be possible for new cities to be made up of such prefab housing furniture, whose surface can also be used as a terrace?

Agoraphobia: the flip side of compaction pressure

In addition to the question of how to deal with the millions of people flocking to metropolitan areas, the issue of new forms of housing also entails the question of what happens in the places those millions are leaving: in the countryside, in the emptying rural regions and regions affected by structural change. There, the problem is not a lack but rather an oversupply of space for those who have stayed behind—and this unexpected agoraphobic situation likewise contains the seed of a new culture of habitation. In Detroit, nearly 80,000 empty homes were to be torn down or fixed up. Numerous publications describe Detroit's urban renewal since 2000 and what compaction and renewal in abandoned office districts and residential areas could look like—from the cultivation of wasteland by grassroots urban farmers and community activists to the conversion of vacant hotels into much-needed affordable housing.[16] "Almost all of the projects involve the renovation of long-vacant historic commercial and industrial buildings, many dating from the early 20th century and featuring the kind of heavily ornamented terra-cotta façades and floors with relatively small square footage that are especially attractive to residential developers."[17] As a result, "businesses are relocating downtown, and people can afford to live closer to where they work." A case in point is the East German town of Leinefelde.

In 1961 a cotton mill was built there, employing up to 4,500 people. Between 1966 and 1989 numerous *plattenbau* buildings went up in Leinefelde to accommodate the town population, which increased from 6,658 to 15,526 in the fifteen-year period from 1970 until 1985. Following the collapse of the local industry in 1989, the population figure dropped dramatically. How was one to deal with the *plattenbau* building stock that had been hastily thrown up in boom times and designed for expansion? Several architects, including Stefan Forster from Munich, have adapted the modular structures to the new demographic situation, literally decon-

Physicists' quarter development, Leinefelde (Meier-Scupin & Petzet)

structing them and removing layers, floors, and elements to create urban villas with roof terraces. Aside from this artful adaptation, this mimicry of the bourgeois housing ideal of the Bauhaus villa by the ruins of socialist utopian expansionism, there is, however, another way of dealing with the vacant buildings: to leave them as they are on the outside, but hollow them out on the inside, remove walls and ceilings, and then to try out new forms of collective dwelling, allowing those forms to freely embed themselves in the new, open expanses of their spaces; to live and work there like in lofts, and to use the vertically and horizontally porosified structure as studios, workshops, residential communities, gigantic start-up offices, emergency shelters—as a kind of Noah's Ark/Centre Pompidou/village.

Dismantled elements of the apartment blocks were already used there to erect flat-roofed shop buildings that were placed in the previously desolate open spaces between the residential blocks, where they were complemented by a Japanese garden. Taking this system a conceptual step further, the obsolete elements could be used to build a kind of medina quarter in which other, new uses could embed themselves—a potential urban compaction model for both shrinking and growing cities.

Such a medina quarter for a *plattenbau* complex has been proposed for one of the largest prefab, concrete-slab building developments in the German capital by June 14, a young Berlin architecture office. The flat-roofed structure that is to be built in the open spaces between the *plattenbau* buildings consists of three levels. The lowest of these only has delicate concrete legs that carry the structure; glass walls serve to partition small offices, between which a lively maze of alleys and spaces is created—a modern medina quarter of sorts where one can also imagine shops, cafés, workshops, kindergartens, and start-up offices. The more public spaces of the dwellings are located here as well; staircases then lead up to the second floor, where the bedrooms and private areas are.

The spaces receive sunlight and air through light wells, which each have a tree growing in them, as well as through atriums. Each room on the second floor opens to such an atrium, which is concealed from view, where people can have their morning coffee, let a small child play, or barbecue with friends. For a larger group of friends, one can also go up from the dwellings to the roof, which is a communal roof terrace, a raised park for all residents. The architects are basically stacking three landscapes: a work landscape on the ground floor, a dwelling landscape consisting of private cells on the second floor, and a recreation and park landscape on the roof. The ground level is relatively public; the glass walls are easy to dismantle and can be rearranged to create ever new spaces for varying uses, like in a micro-Metabolist game. The second level is extremely private—no windows to the outside, only to the atrium. And then the roof is a space for all; the communal area diffuses upwards, as it were, through a filter.

Urban living project,
Karl-Marx-Allee, Berlin (June 14)

June 14 has radicalized the atmosphere of the spaces: the privacy of the dwelling becomes decidedly more private, and the dwellings which only have windows going to the interior courtyard become snugger and more secure, whereas the workspaces and kitchens become more flexible and open; this way, dwelling is both more open and more protected. The apartment sizes vary between 615 square feet (one-bedroom apartment) and 1,840 square feet (seven-room apartment). The private areas of the home, the bedrooms and the bathroom, are located upstairs, and the more public spaces, such as kitchen or office, on the ground floor.

The functions of "working," "dwelling," and "relaxing" are no longer separated horizontally: during lunch break, people can go to their apartments and sleep or to the roof and into the sun to gather with others. The design thus brings back a city feeling in a new form. The architecture also allows occupants to rent out part of their space (the areas on the ground floor) as offices, thus enabling those with low incomes to stay in the city as well. The form in this case is also an economic construction to preserve the social mix of the city.

Such houses, if they were built, would fundamentally change the concept of living in the city. They would bring back into the city many of those who move to the periphery in exasperation, because they do not find the quiet, the greenery, a space of their own in the current housing association dreariness. The housing associations and the Berlin *Liegenschaftsfonds*, or real estate fund, are one hundred percent publicly owned. Hence the only thing that is missing for such architecture to be realized is a political signal or, alternatively, a private initiative.

Architects to the barricades: self-empowerment

Another question this book poses is how architects can step out of the passive role of actors who sit around like private detectives waiting for a client to come through the door, and become active city builders; how especially the numerous brilliant young architects presented in this book can realize their ideas in an act of architectural self-empowerment, without waiting for the transformation of an inert building bureaucracy and a building industry that is reluctant to change. The examples of joint building ventures in Germany point the way for bottom-up strategies to change urban districts.

Most of the projects presented in this volume are houses and not cities—which raises the question of whether the housing problem of the coming years and decades, when billions of people will need to be housed, can still be coped with through architecture at all and whether the concern with small houses is not of rather marginal importance in this context. Suggesting that such a concern may still be worthwhile is the fact that the major aesthetic and social upheavals in the modern history of architecture first manifested themselves in the microcosm of the dwelling cell—in Le Corbusier's 1929 Villa Savoye, for instance, or in Mies van der Rohe's 1951 Farnsworth House, which is no bigger than an average American double garage. Such projects contained the seed for all large-scale projects that followed; the residence is often the first concentrate of a new architectural theory, a new concept of space, a social utopia.

The Occupy movement has also made its mark on urban theory and the theory of habitation: a number of new publications deal with the importance of squares for the protest movements in Iran, North Africa, and Ukraine. Architecture departments study grassroots organizations and the participatory models[18] through which citizens, on a local level, demand sovereignty over the design of public spaces. But here, too, the language is to a large degree ideologically informed: participation sounds great, but is "citizen involvement" through "participation procedures" in designing a street really an involvement in political decision-making processes or, rather, its opposite: sidelining through decorative participationism? What would real involvement in the issue of the kind of spaces one would want to live in—and live in together—look like?

The concern with housing is often criticized as secondary by the activists of public space: political architecture is equated with "claiming back" public space, democracy with demonstration, and dwelling with privacy and depoliticization. But what happens before people take to the streets?—in what spaces do the processes of information, debate, exchange, and dispute take place? Can architecture promote or curb such processes, can it fuel or prevent a basic social ardor? These are questions related to "dwelling," to the private and public spaces that are just as much part of the "revival of publicness" as are the occupations of Maidan Square, Tahrir Square, or Zuccotti Park.

This book has two goals: to contribute to the analysis of interests and forces responsible for apartments, houses, and cities looking the way they do today, and to present projects and figures of thought that provide an outlook on how we could rethink publicness and privacy and, as a result, dwell and live differently. Rather than giving final answers, it aims to ask first questions. It is not a treatise against the single-family home, but it does ask why—in view of the factual demographic situation and the ecological and economic problems caused by single-family residences and by housing construction which is planned in defiance of demographics—so few dwellings for other lifestyles exist and what such dwellings could look like.

Few things are as indicative of the state of a society as its spaces: its living rooms, its furniture, its bedrooms, children's rooms, gardens, streets, and squares. For this reason alone it is worth taking a closer look at the house, the square, the city and understanding the power constellations and interests that are at work there, in order to realize what could be different, what new rituals of privacy and publicness have emerged, and what new forms can be developed to accommodate this.

Chapter 1

City and Suburb

The Zombified City

"Living like the Queen of Prussia"
What the new commercials for homes tell us

What could life look like? Like this, for instance: a woman, perhaps in her mid-thirties, wearing cream-colored pants and a gray blazer, rambles through Berlin in the morning hours, passing by the Deutscher Dom cathedral, crossing Gendarmenmarkt, walking past the red awning of the Borchardt restaurant, which—heavy, red, and upscale—projects into the Berlin morning, as if all by itself aspiring to transform the cold center of Berlin into a part of Paris. The woman goes shopping; she is seen on the escalator of Quartier 206, where she disappears into a store. A couple of Louis Vuitton purses can be seen in the store's shopwindow. Now it is afternoon: the woman walks past Schinkel's old museum—strumming and violins can be heard, the sounds plunging like cascades in minor into the depths. The woman enters a restaurant. A man with a wolf-like grin greets her with the snappy upbeatness of a sportscaster. He is wearing an open shirt and a dark suit and grins at her as if wanting to bite her. Obviously, he works in the neighborhood and is meeting his wife here for lunch.

Advertising for the Kronprinzengärten complex in Berlin

Cut: we see the new residential quarter where the woman lives: white façades, muntined windows, green blinds, boxwood trimmed in a round ball shape, the architecture looking as if the architect added some whipped cream-like plaster around the boring flan case to make the whole look a little more like Art Deco. Oddly, a carriage is parked in front of the house; the woman seems to be hosting a just defrosted Alexander von Humboldt.

We follow the woman into the apartment; inside, everything is cream-colored and dull blue; a reading chair is beckoning behind the fireplace and we see a gramophone whose horn seems to be inaudibly blaring something.

Located on the roof of the house is an elongated swimming pool with a view across to the Friedrichswerder Church. The woman goes swimming until it gets dark; her high heels can be seen at the edge of the pool. Later she meets the well-toothed man for dinner. This time she is wearing a gown that makes her look even paler. She raises an oversize red wineglass to the man, while outside the city lights go on; based on the way they sit at the table, it is as if they were keeping a watchful eye on one another. It is easy to imagine how, a few months later, she will be seeing a therapist and he will be seeing another woman, or vice versa. But before it gets to that, the short film, a promo of real estate developer Bauwert advertising the "Kronprinzengärten" at Friedrichswerder Church, an 85-million-euro residential complex with thirty luxury condos in the center of Berlin, is already over.

The new luxury real estate projects have given rise to a new film genre—that of the commercial architecture film, which, usually accessible on the company's website, uses sophisticated technology to showcase life as it could be in an (as yet) unbuilt house. This particular one is a horror film: it shows an empty existence. The woman is not doing anything: rather than going to the museum, she just walks past it; she does not work and apparently has no job nor any friends, just her husband. Her day consists of shopping, swimming, and waiting for the husband, a man who can only be found in restaurants; even for him the apartment is obviously too boring.

The film's setting, central Berlin, was where, after the fall of the wall, the excessive epicenter of the city was located, the world of illegal clubs, extreme physical exertion, drugs, deep basses—of pale, sweat-soaked figures being flushed past the construction sites of office blocks by the end of the night; the ear-deafening omnipresence of techno; the partied-out and sweat-soaked and dirtied-up and tattered. And here, of all places, is where a world of creamy dull pleasures is created, as shown in the film—a world in which the most intense experience is the Louis Vuitton purse straps cutting into the flesh.

One could write a sociopolitical theory of the body based on these figures, an anthropomorphosis of capital that shows how an economic system seeps into the sensibility and the shape of bodies: we see two individuals here who are defined by the curious concurrency of a need to relax and self-discipline, as found in yoga: the woman, silently, pliantly, and doggedly fighting off decay, and the man, a jovially grinning wellness wolf with marathon-toughened calves. It is impossible to imagine these people screaming, partying loudly, goofing off, wasting time, fighting, laughing—all they seem to do is silently and energetically carry on a cold marble existence they "want to create" for themselves, its highlight being the long bath in the rooftop pool.

"Continue the story—the next chapter can be written by you," it says in the film's closing credits: buy an apartment and you can become like the two shown here. It is meant to be a promise, but it feels like a threat.

The promotional film advertising the "Lenbach-Gärten," a luxury housing complex in Munich with a price per square foot ranging between 418 and 930 euros, offers more of the same. The "Frankonia Premium Stadtquartier"—built by real estate developer Frankonia Eurobau, whose development portfolio includes the "Sophienterrassen" in Hamburg, the "Klostergärten" in Münster, and the "Heinrich-Heine-Gärten" in Düsseldorf—is said to exude the "magic of grandeur" and "intimate comfort." According to the Frankonia website, "spacious piazzettas lend the Frankonia Urban Quarters their special urban charm. The wrought-iron fences not only serve security purposes, but also delight the viewer's eyes with their classical proportions based on the golden ratio." The commercial can be taken apart like a riddle poem: it is about double safety—

from burglars, from the present and change—provided by the certitude of classical proportion and the golden ratio. It evokes the nostalgic image of the Italian piazza and its "urban charm"—a square whose urbanity used to be defined by its general accessibility and the absence of classically proportioned fences.

Yet another promotional video can be found on the Internet, one in which an unshaven man with a high-pitched voice speaks to the people of Berlin. Judging by his accent the man is French and what he says suggests he is the villain of a new James Bond movie. People will be surprised, this man says. He claims to be speaking for an organization called "Yoo," which indeed appears like the negation of 007 with a stylized Martini glass at the beginning instead of a figure seven at the end. When figures like this appear in Bond movies, nothing less than the world itself is at risk, and a city like Berlin will not exist much longer. And this is exactly how it is—even if the man speaking is merely the designer Philippe Starck, whose ideas have so far threatened primarily the world of chairs and functional lemon squeezers, albeit quite successfully. For Berlin he developed, together with Peach Property Group, the "Yoo" real estate project: right on the Spree River, adjacent to the theater that is home to the Berlin Ensemble, a ten-story, formally conservative building is going up, featuring a spa, an indoor pool, and other amenities that until now have been rare in Berlin, and in this building ninety-five condos are for sale at an average price per square foot of 810 euros. No need to bring furniture: the apartments are furnished upon request. Regarding the interior, the threat uttered by Philippe Starck in the video applies: "Nothing is normal, everything is a creation"— a creation, that is, from the headquarters of design-idea hell: the chandelier looks as if it has been produced by a raging beaver with a tail full of cement, and in the middle of the space stands a wheelbarrow that serves as a chair.

We are all part of a cultural family, Starck explains in the architect's film, a family that can be divided into four stylistic subsets, which correspond to the four interior design categories of the apartments in the "Yoo" building: "Classic," "Minimal," "Nature," and "Culture." "Your wife will love it," Starck says (apparently the promo is aimed exclusively at men). "Those who opt for the Culture

Style savor luxury," the Peach Property Group explains in a dossier. "He or she could be a collector, for example." The theater people and the artists who until recently lived next door, sometimes using the square for performances or picnics, are rubbing their eyes: where just a short while ago there used to be culture, there is now *Culture*.

Art plays an important role in the new real estate projects, since no one who is buying an apartment in Berlin for over a million euros wants to hear that the neighborhood consists of twenty mansions and fourteen guard dogs that pee on the rhododendrons in the front yard. Buyers want to participate in the so-called bubbling cultural life that is said to define Berlin's center—a center that is, as the sales brochure for "Yoo" states, populated by "self-assured successful people and young art stars in waiting," the implicit promise to future "Yoo" residents being that they may even be able to release those young talents from their wait state. Beckoning with the purchase of one of the overpriced condos is a future as a popular patron and/or collector, an exciting life in bohemian circles.

It has rightly been pointed out that gentrification also has positive aspects and that there is an unsympathetic, populist aggression toward anything that endangers Berlin's dallying foot-dragging, a hatred of everything that looks like money and style. Yet the new properties in the city center do not, in spite of all claims and wishful thinking to the contrary, signal a return of middle-class culture into a center devastated by socialism. What it does signal is cynical real estate capitalism exploiting and consummating the woes of antiurban command economy. The new buildings with their synthetic old-city flavor have nothing in common with the lifestyle epitomized in Berlin by, say, the upper-class building at no. 15 Bleibtreustrasse, where the art dealer Alfred Flechtheim lived until 1933.

Still, the developers of the "Kronprinzengärten" do bank on the appeal of art as well: the planned structures include a gallery building, a "house of art" with ceiling heights of up to 15.7 feet. With the self-confidence of a drunken pub-goer, the new structures edge within 16 feet of their neighbor, Schinkel's famous Friedrichswerder Church, where during construction the plaster from the ceiling came crashing to the floor. At the time, the Prussian Cultural Heritage Foundation issued a statement that for safety reasons all sculptures had to be removed from the church.

Yet the new construction projects do not just, in the good old ways of gentrification, replace the simple and makeshift with a more affluent middle-class life: they zombify the city, resurrecting what they supplanted—the studios, the small art spaces, the improvised, the provisional—as a value-enhancing, exhilarating image. The new city recreates as fiction what it has just displaced: the artist is to lend the neighborhood the flavor of urban resistance; he is allowed to return, as an impersonator of himself, to the place of his displacement, to keep the residents from recognizing the sterility they have brought with them.

Where too much obvious capitalism prevails, calls for art arise— as in the new development area behind Berlin's Hauptbahnhof, or central station, a neighborhood blocked up by tangled office and hotel buildings, where the mayor of Berlin would have liked to build a new art gallery. Putting art spaces as value-enhancing decorative cherries on top of commercial real estate projects has become fashionable. Wilhelm Brandt, the former press spokesman of real estate developer Vivico, described art as bait to lure important people into the city: "It is like the sausage and cold cut counter: the more choice the better."[1]

Zombification: 40 Bond Street and the cynicism of the post-urban city

The zombification of the city center is not a European phenomenon. Manhattan's Lower East Side is seeing high-end condo buildings going up in places where there used to be punk clubs, with real estate agents unwaveringly advertising the neighborhoods' "bohemian character"—a character that is in danger of disappearing not least because of the new construction. Accordingly, the few remaining punks and underground artists vent their displeasure and cover the new buildings with angry graffiti, which the owners do not, mind you, accept as art, but rather decry as vandalism.

The sociologically most interesting of the new buildings in the Bowery is the luxury apartment block at 40 Bond Street, which was built by the Swiss architecture firm Herzog & de Meuron for hotelier-developer Ian Schrager.

There have been protests against the building, which stands for the gentrification of one of the last social oases and the final displacement of the median-income population from Manhattan. This was one reason why the architects had a bizarre structure raised between the street and the building itself—it looks like a mixture between a fence and sculpture and is, in fact, both: a barrier against the real bohemian world of the punks and an emblem of the perceived underground affiliation of the new tenants, who are paying steep prices for the luxury apartments in this building (according to the industry information service "The real deal," the monthly rent is said to be well above $20,000).

40 Bond Street, New York
(Herzog & de Meuron)

The fence in front of the façade has a labyrinthine curving shape that looks as if Jackson Pollock had painted it in the air with liquid, rapid-hardening lead. On the website we learn that the building is "New York City graffiti-inspired"—that is, it derives its form from the kind of graffiti that in the past was all over the Bowery and which can still be seen on the façades of the new buildings as a sign of protest against the gentrification of neighborhoods. Once word got around that this fence was really a graffito congealed into a sculpture, it became the symbol of an equally brilliant and cynical assimilation strategy of the gentrifiers, a sneering salute from the new property owners to the sprayers, whose own form of protest now faces them as a fortification shielding the façade from being sprayed.

Cast in aluminum and with a length of 128 feet and a height of 23 feet, the fence achieves both: it advertises the flair of the subculture, while at the same time keeping it at arm's length. It transforms the anarchic energy of the bohemian punk scene into an artwork and this artwork is at the same time the best conceivable protection against the real resentment of the culture it references. It frustrates the actual anger that is armed with spray cans, for any attempt to spray on this barrier inevitably leads to the paint being scattered in the air; it never reaches the actual façade behind it. Like prewashed jeans, the building flirts with the aesthetics of damage, thereby converting any conceivable protest into part of its design: the aesthetic of the graffiti fence absorbs all forms of ideological opposition and turns them into an ornament of its triumph.

The overfurnished city: strategies of control

The fence at 40 Bond St. is just one example of a new form of furnishing the city with objects of control and partition that deftly deny their defensive character. Overgrown parks are redesigned and furnished with bicycle lanes, benches, plantings of flowers, small fences, and playground and fitness equipment. One may welcome this overfurnishing of former wasteland and open space as an improvement of a city's quality of life, but it can also be seen as a subtle form of control of public space, leaving no room for unrest, demonstrations, marches, or riotous assemblies of any significance.

When looking for the causes underlying the drab appearance of cities, the failure of institutions that could contain the proliferation of profit-oriented low-end buildings and luxury ghettos besetting open spaces stands out. These institutions include, more than anything, public authorities—in Berlin, for instance, the Berliner Liegenschaftsfonds, a real estate fund that far too often and for far too long has been accepting the highest bids, even if this entails high long-term consequential costs, meaning the desolation of entire city districts and historically developed structures. Instead, people rejoice over the profitable sale of land to private players when the city could have emerged as the inventor and builder of new social spaces and new forms of housing. The mayor of the Berlin district of Charlottenburg-Wilmersdorf, Reinhard Naumann, enthused over the "Rosengärten" project: "The 'Rosengärten' provide new housing in [our] district where demand is very high due to a major influx of residents and an increasing number of small households. The realization of the 'Rosengärten' is an important step to meet demand, especially for a wide range of rental apartments in the district." By this he meant the demand for upscale real estate; the need for centrally located, affordable apartments that would allow families, students, and elderly people to live in central parts of the city seems to have been less of a concern here. Hence it is above all politics with its short-sighted, for-profit sale of municipal property that contributes to making city centers desolate.[2]

From place of promise to security zone

In nineteenth-century novels and songs, as well as in films and paintings, the big city is a chaotic, overcrowded, confusing and dark open space full of perils and opportunities—on the one hand, the well-founded fear of literally going under in the crowded streets and, on the other, the promise of a glittering world full of possibility. Petula Clark in her song "Downtown," the anthem of bored suburbanites, still celebrated the city center as a glittering, sparkling promise, where the lights are brighter, the music louder, and the people friendlier. It would be wrong to romanticize this idea of the city and take it at face value: cities have always reflected commercial interests; they were never cheerful playgrounds. Even so, something has changed in the approach to urban spaces.

The new cities are not shaped by the idea of promise, but rather by the ideal of protection against threats: automobile traffic has been minimized, empty spaces have been cluttered up with street furniture, and everything has been pedestrianized and shopping-optimized. The "Other"—in 1970s and 1980s philosophy and urban design theories the projection surface of the wildest imagination and a promise—has turned into a threat. One might ask if the tendency to think about everything from the perspective of the possibility of death is a symptom of a society that is no longer predicated on a concept of freedom, like in the 1970s, but rather on a notion of security. Data retention and the surveillance of public space are largely accepted—because they increase safety. The encounter with others in public space has become a fearful notion and is imagined as potentially life-threatening. Terror, AIDS, crashes: the man wearing a turban could be an assassin; the nice person at the bar could carry a dangerous disease; there is a constant fear of collisions, muggings, gang attacks, civil commotions of all kind.

What these new cities look like, guided as they are by the promise of profit, principles of minimizing dangers, calming traffic, and other ways of casketing urban energies, is exemplified by Hamburg's "Hafencity."

The myth of the economic imperative
Hamburg's "Hafencity"

There is a shortage of affordable housing in Hamburg as well. High hopes were pinned on the "Hafencity," one of the largest urban building projects in Germany. Several promising housing cooperatives had already formed there and if one had continued condensing the new city in this manner, it could have become a vibrant part of town. Instead, the so-called Überseequartier, or Overseas Quarter, was built, a new neighborhood where about 7,000 people are supposed to work. Eight hundred million euros were invested, among other things in an "Überseeboulevard" whose brick wall canyons tend to evoke the etymological origin of the word "boulevard" in German war vocabulary, that is, of a bulwark or bastion. What has happened here? Why was the most beautiful waterfront location used to create a pedestrian zone that one could not imagine more desolate?

The answer is simple: because the aim was to create above all office space. It was argued that a mixed, compartmentalized residential area with affordable apartments and gardens near the water is a beautiful utopian, yet unrealistic dream. Offices were said to be needed in order for the whole thing to pay off. Yet the claimed economic necessity was a mistake: while there is a shortage of housing in Hamburg, about ten million square feet of office space was already vacant before construction even began, almost four million of that in the Hafencity alone, and the oversupply drove down prices.

Economically in particular, the consequences were disastrous: the Hamburg senate had pledged to take over 485,000 square feet from the investor of a commercial complex, apparently because it feared that the image of a flourishing commercial district could otherwise collapse. Now the public authorities had to live up to its promise. After looking in vain for another buyer, the city had to step in as lessee. At first there were plans to move the Central District Office to the Hafencity, which the district politicians, however, considered too expensive: they would have had to subsidize the Hafencity rental market by paying a leasing rate of 161 instead of 86 euros per square foot. Eventually, the Hamburg Ministry of Economic Affairs was to move in, but its employees protested vehemently against the remote location.

Hafencity, Hamburg

What happened here was not the global economy pouring money into public coffers that authorities could then put to beneficial use; rather, public authorities supported the image of a flourishing economy at the cost of a desolation of public space. The Überseequartier in Hafencity soon became a Potemkin village of the global economy, a simulacrum of urbanity, a cityscape instead of a city.

More than anything, it is the subordination to the supposedly inevitable imperative of the economic that shapes the current image of cities. The "heart of the Hafencity" was sold early on to a German-Dutch consortium, and the attempts by city planners to still breathe life into the area have been limited to urban cosmetics: architecture is allowed to provide the homey camouflage for the forms that commercial interests have taken. The office blocks were thus given a nostalgic local color in the form of brick façades, and because people in Hamburg always fret that things look too staid, the architects were allowed to incorporate a couple of meaningless visual turbulences. Erick van Egeraat's Sumatra House looks as if a rusty oil tanker has been cut apart and recycled as façade decoration. The economic disaster is memorialized by the visual ruin and the heart of the Hafencity is allowed to look like what, socially and in terms of urban planning, it actually is: a heap of rubble.

What notion of society and what priorities the marketers of the new city district have is illustrated best by the Hafencity website, where a new school called Katharinenschule is pitched not as a place of humanist education but rather as a manager mill for future business leaders. "The children," we read, "enjoy their break on what is most likely the city's highest schoolyard, which offers a spectacular panorama, and in doing so they learn an important entrepreneurial virtue: farsightedness."[3] All the more embarrassing then that everything the young entrepreneur sees from up here had to be state-financed.

A theory of overcrowding
Dreams of the Romanisches Café

What is so drab about Berlin's Friedrichstraße, Hamburg's Übersee-boulevard, and all the new synthetic urban development plans? Those newly constructed buildings that line the streets like filing folders? The nighttime desolation indicating that the place is dominated by offices rather than apartments? And what makes the intersection at Bahnhof Zoo where the "Romanisches Café" is located—a café that adopted its name from a famous predecessor—so depressingly dismal?

It has not always been so utterly drab here. There is a painting from 1910 that shows glitter; the sky over Kurfürstendamm is sulfur-yellow from the lights of the city, rather than black; the light is reflected on the wet pavement and one cannot even see the way toward the Romanisches Café through the throngs of people shoving along Kurfürstendamm and toward the Bahnhof Zoo train station. This is what it was like in front of the Romanisches Café in 1910 when the artist Adolf Müller-Cassel created the eponymous painting. The writer and journalist Egon Erwin Kisch and the painter Max Slevogt had a stammtisch here; Sylvia von Harden, the model for a famous Otto Dix painting, and the satirist Kurt Tucholsky were among the regulars, as were the poets Else Lasker-Schüler und Gottfried Benn. Mascha Kaléko wrote some of her most beautiful poems here ("Half past one. So late! / Time to count the guests /

I am packing my optimism / In this city of four million souls / A soul seems scarce indeed." The year 1933, when Mascha Kaléko wrote this poem, spelled the end for the Romanisches Café. The building was eventually gutted in a November 1943 air raid. Seventy years later the new Zoofenster tower was opened, which houses the Waldorf Astoria Hotel—and the so-called new Romanisches Café. Yet at the opening you couldn't even tell until the last moment that there was, in fact, a café here: elements essential to a café, such as a door, were missing. You had to steal into the new Romanisches Café through a side entrance of the hotel. Similar to the showroom of a fertilizer dealer, the windows facing the street were blocked by big containers that had disoriented grass growing in them, and from the ceiling, neon spotlights, like those in a hospital, beat down on the plates, as if one were meant to operate on the cakes rather than eat them.

The new Romanisches Café showed what is missing in Berlin, and not just in Berlin. Whether we look at Müller-Cassel's painting or read Kästner on the "infernal bustle" at the old café, we always get the impression of overcrowding, of an extreme, chaotic super-compression of the city. Perhaps what made the city so vibrant was not just the "urban spaces" of the old Berlin—as Berlin city planners thought after 1989, leading to coarse efforts of reconstruction in the form of hard-edge boxes—but rather the overcrowding which, unfortunately, had not been reconstructed along with it: façades wildly leaning into the street with baroque balconies that had armies of caryatids attached to them, and underneath that a hustle and bustle, a chaos of carriages, people, kiosks—a culture of public space that emerged because so many people were moving to Berlin, and who went to the cafés because apartments were too cramped.

Those who step out of the new building of the Romanisches Café at 10 p.m. find themselves in a wasteland with some light added to it by the blue neon tubes of the Karstadt store, the red ones of the Beate Uhse store, and the green ones of the "Wursterei," a sausage shack. At least the neon writing on the train station has been renewed, so that it no longer reads "_ _ _logischer Garten."

This impression of desertedness also has something to do with the city's population density; too few people live in the center. The Berlin of the 1920s, which on old photographs appears as a glittering, sparkling jumble of coffeehouses, neon signs, traffic lights, streetcars, horse-drawn vehicles, fur coats, automobiles, hats, electricity, hustle and bustle, love, and cigar smoke, was the product of insane compression. In 1877, Berlin's population reached one million, by 1905 the population had doubled, and by 1920 it was four million. Berlin was now the third-largest city in the world after London and New York. Emigrants flocked to Berlin and overcrowded the city, and this overcrowdedness was its richness: three times the number of people actually planned for were living on Friedrichstrasse and in the areas where today "Yoo" and the "Kronprinzengärten" are being constructed. These masses that flocked to the center brought a mix of social strata and cultural rituals with them, a chaotic compression that was the opposite of taking vacant properties in the city center and covering them with upscale, sleek, and zombifying urbanism. Of course, 1920s Berlin also had posh residential buildings. But living right next door to them, behind them, under the roof were people with considerably less money who opened bars and small stores.

In the new residential areas you look in vain for this kind of intermixture and super-compression. Berlin's Friedrichstrasse is suffering from the fact that the urban silhouette—perimeter development, eaves height, façades with proportionally more stone than glass—has been reconstructed (thereby preventing large autistic projects such as the Kudamm-Karree), but the life that once made Friedrichstrasse a dense, bubbling place has not been restored. The reconstruction of this area in the center of a city also points to more comprehensive structural woes of state building policies: formal shells are recreated to win back a lost, vibrant city feeling, a lost atmosphere, without understanding that it is necessary to examine the structural conditions of this atmosphere and, maybe, build very different forms in order to arrive at a similar urban atmosphere. It would have benefited Friedrichstrasse if from the beginning, rather than banking on maximization of profits by developing office space, plans had called for extremely compressed, popular residential development as well: soon cafés, small stores, and movie theaters would have moved into the neighborhood. The way things are, though, Friedrichstrasse is a Berlin version of La Défense in the custom-made suit of the old European city: an office district in a nostalgic mold. Closer examination of most façades leaves no doubt that what has established itself here is not a mixed center but rather an office world where form follows efficiency: instead of displaying the wealth of detail and almost hysterical overdecoration of old *Gründerzeit* façades, the office buildings stand in file like petrified ring binders. The city is a reflection of the construction industry's pursuit of returns. The state responds to this by introducing mere cosmetic changes, such as stipulating a certain small percentage of subsidized housing.

It is also possible, of course, that the planners of the new cities really do not want to return to the ideal of the unruly, overcrowded city. Perhaps the ideal is not the glittering, cosmopolitan, confusing, dangerous, seductive, wild, loud, steaming, blurred, sharp, shrill, soft, lost, ice-cold, and overheated metropolis of modernity, the city of peril and promise, but rather the opposite: the feudally lukewarm, small-town premodern city that is evoked by the old carriage in the promo for the "Kronprinzengärten," a complex whose name, Crown Prince Gardens, suggests exactly that: the city of the safe idyll. The two models are antithetical: the city as a place of adventure, of encountering the unfamiliar and the confusing, and the city as a tidy, spick-and-span, manageable vision of order. The way the Berliner Liegenschaftsfonds advertised a large city-owned piece of land near the Charlottenburg Palace gardens to potential bidders is telling: as "land for the development of high-end housing" under the slogan "Living like Sophie Charlotte," the Prussian queen.

Metamorphoses of public space
How the airport becomes a shopping mall

The commercial transformation of public spaces is not a phenomenon that is limited to squares and streets in city centers. What once defined cities reappears as a strange mirage, a fata morgana of steel, outside of the cities: airports in particular are turning from places that are about providing as expeditious a departure as possible into places where one can—and indeed is supposed to—spend days among hotels, massage centers, boutiques, and restaurants. In the very places modernity invented for the purpose of accelerating circumstances, life decelerates into the forcibly flâneur-like.

Built in 1974 by the German architectural firm gmp, Berlin Tegel Airport was an acceleration structure: a large hexagonal building onto which airplanes can directly dock by means of fourteen jet bridges, while travelers can be dropped off directly in front of a particular check-in counter in the terminal's inner court. It may be that such a design is no longer possible today, but the potential terror threat alone does not explain why travelers who are forced to show up at check-in at an absurdly early time must now wander through endless shopping malls at the new airport, where they will indiscriminately buy things just to fill the time.

If the new Berlin airport does in fact ever open, it will be a place of strategic delay. The engineers of consciousness, who eventually have to sell the features of such structures to the public, would rather call it "deceleration," because that is considered socially desirable. People do not like speeders and tailgaters and turbo-capitalism; they want quiet zones and retreat. Yet what is overlooked in the process is that deceleration, the apotheosis of the loiterer turned epicure, is by no means an act of rehumanization, but rather the true pitch of the very so-called turbo-capitalism that it is ostensibly pitted against. By now, wellness centers, yoga spaces, low-fat gourmet food restaurants, and other upscale self-consolation facilities are available at the airport, and this metamorphosis of the airport into a stroller's maze with well-hidden departure options is quite simply predicated on the profits that can be made with the promise of comprehensive self-optimization through relaxation and culinary art.

As the Moodie Report and the annual reports of London Heathrow and other airports point out, "non-aviation areas" are by now one of the largest sources of revenue for airport operators. Fifty percent of the revenue of major international airports is no longer generated by passenger fees and freight charges but by what is called, even in contemporary business German, "airport retailing" and what, at over 1,200 euros per square foot, yields considerably more than any regular urban shopping center. For example, according to "Research Network Airport City Facts 2012," the Hugo Boss store at Frankfurt Airport achieved a "surface area productivity of 1,858 euros per square foot," and "rents topping at 95 euros per square foot are no longer uncommon in airport retailing." In Athens, Greece, and Portland, Oregon, the airports even have retail parks with Ikea stores attached to them.

Based on this alone it is understandable that retail space, which at Tegel was around 35,000 square feet, is to cover about 236,800 square feet at Berlin Brandenburg International and that delay is the very essence of new transportation infrastructure.

The mutation of the airport from a temple of acceleration into a shopping maze with peripheral departure option is not the result of safety requirements or general growth, but rather of the economic transformation of public spaces. With the metamorphosis of airports into highly profitable shopping centers, airport architecture, too, reaches new lows: the new airports look like what they are: glorified shopping malls where one is forced to slow down on the way from the entrance to the airplane and stay forever in coffee bars, restaurants, shops, and lounges. The new airports abolish the idea of flying, the fastest possible mode of transportation: the aesthetic promise is gone and so is the real velocity.

Through the addition of urban décor the commercial patronizing of the air traveler awaiting departure in endless shopping arcades is turned into a fancy "city experience" where the boundaries between the public sphere and intimacy become peculiarly soft. Under the overarching metal roofs of these malls a strangely hybrid intermixing of intimate and public spaces is taking place; weary business travelers sleep in living-room-like lounge corners and waiting areas, while next to them people are ordering coffee, buying magazines and small presents. In between there are no walls. It is as if the front of a house had been removed and with it the distinction between private and public. Understood as a place accessible to all residents of a community, the piazza at this mall is, of course, not really a public square, but rather the fiction of a square that is public only for the privileged world of air travelers. And what is all the more interesting is that this very exclusive location cannot but reference the premodern "market square idyll" from whose essential feature, general accessibility, it has departed.

Some architecture theoreticians suggest that in terms of layout, the architecture of airports and shopping malls is modeled on classic city centers and in terms of their concentration, on places of trade. There is indeed some evidence for this, but nowadays we can find the reverse as well: aseptically well-planned city centers that resemble the shopping zones of major airports. Surveillance cameras everywhere and squares as smooth as glass, forbidding façades, illuminated nooks, the city as an endless sequence of locks that people are pushed through.

Understandably, the cluttering, commercialization, and disinfection of urban centers in such massive form entails evocations of an unobstructed idyll. The appearance of urban centers and airports alone may explain the successes of magazines such as *Landlust* (Country Delight) and *Country Life*, which eulogize life in the countryside and, as consolation, offer all kinds of strategies for making one's home cozier.

Suburbia

War of ideals

The forlornness of the economized city centers continues in the suburbs: because the city does not offer any affordable living space for families, they migrate to the housing mush at the outskirts. Yet even there, in the new building plots the municipalities release for construction, things are already very tight.

Many of those building plots suffer aesthetic massacres. Because the overextended communities cede development planning to private investors, design guidelines are lacking, and because no agreements are reached, one architectural design batters the next. Thus we encounter, next to one another in the smallest of spaces: the shrunken version of a Bauhaus home that calls for other white boxes as neighbors; an elaborate half-timber house that would need a field with horses or an old windmill as neighbors, rather than white boxes, so as not to lose its impact—yet instead, a low-end house with plastic windows and apricot-colored insulating plaster is stuck right next to it. Such developments are awful not just because their architecture does not adhere to particular normative design rules and notions of good taste, but because they fail immanently. The owner of the elaborate half-timber house is all worked up, because when looking out of his living-room window he sees not the countryside idyll that had prompted him to move to the outskirts in the first place, but rather the cheap Bauhaus box whose owner collects various flashy stainless-steel appliances that to him seem like modern design. The owner of the white box, in turn, cannot bear the look of the "nostalgic" half-timber house and the painted forest idylls on its garage wall, while the owner of the zero-energy build-

Kladow district (near Berlin)

ing covered in apricot-colored insulating plaster stares irately at the ATV that enables the owner of the half-timber house to indulge his countryside dreams. This is a war of ideals in which each ideal cancels out the others. These developments as a whole have objectively failed and should fall within the scope of defacement clauses found in building codes, if only because none of the residents are thrilled with them, since they all perceive them as a more or less tolerable compromise.

The extremely low-cost boxes that are built by solid-house construction companies no longer have anything in common with classic houses. They have to be cheap, but because the suppliers of solid homes and their crews still want to make as much money off them as possible, they save wherever they can. As a result, the houses tend to have hardly any roof overhang, tiny windows made of the cheapest materials, and walls plastered on the fly, as man hours cost money too.

"Tee-hee, I live in a solid house."

Our model house is located in the southern part of the city, not far from the highway, beyond the traffic circle where the road to Glasow branches off, and beyond the intersection where the freshly plastered, lemon-colored house with a pointed roof stands, which houses the "Imbisseck Borussia" snack bar. In front of the model house are fir trees, hedges, a green twin-wire mesh fence, a black Volkswagen Touareg. The street on which the model home is located is, as of late, called "Zum Storchennest" (At the Stork's Nest); previously called Feldstrasse, it had to be renamed when the communities merged—for the same reason Goethestrasse is now called Bachstrasse, because they already had Goethe in the neighboring locality, but not Bach.

The model house stands on the left, its façade painted a color reminiscent of mealy apricots or a Bellini cocktail. A sign welcomes visitors: "It is good that you are comparing solid houses!" Underneath are pictures of the types of houses the franchise company Town & Country offers: the "Landhaus"—or country home—model with a half-hip roof; the "Bungalow" model; the "Wintergartenhaus" model; the "Lichthaus"—or house of light—model with more windows. Our model house is a "Flair 113"; a plaque informs us that this model is "Germany's best-selling brand home." The salesperson is waiting in the hallway; he wears a black shirt with the name of his company printed in orange on its collar. Pictures of dozens of similar houses are hanging in the hallway; above, on slips of paper cut out in the shape of little clouds, we read the handwritten words "Träume wurden Wirklichkeit" (Dreams have become reality).

The house is furnished as if it were lived in: curry-colored leather sofas, shells on the edge of the vanity basin in the bathroom, the toilet lid covered with yellow terrycloth. The white plastic windows—with double glazing—have spindly muntin bars that, rather than being glued on as in the past, lie in between the panes. "That makes it easier for your wife to clean," the salesperson says, "and it still looks beautiful." Would it also be possible to order wooden windows, with matching wooden blinds? "Why would you want wooden windows?" the salesman asks. Looks better, no? "Theoretically, it can be done, but that would be free planning and a different price! You could also get windows with a wooden look, which would be much less maintenance!" A young couple is sitting on the curry-colored sofa, going through calculations for their dream house: including a bay, they are already at 156,000 euros, not counting a fireplace and the kitchen. The "Flair 113" house model can be ordered with numerous special accessories, like a car; the base price is low. Why is that? "You know," the salesman explains, "the Ytong plant nearby sells half of its stones to us." So you get a discount?

Model house,
Flair 113 series

"That is to be expected, yes." On the bookshelves upstairs are folders listing the "cooperation partners": the Küchentreff company for kitchen manufacturing, the Lenk company for groundwork and structural engineering, the Loberg company for the gardens. Hanging next to the shelves is a certificate of the licenser, Town & Country, "for Organizing Manager Thomas Prigand," who placed "second in the nation in the Town & Country System in 2009" for his

organization management. Another certificate states that in 2005 the same person came in first of all franchisees throughout Germany. Today that person is nowhere to be seen; another salesman guides visitors through the model home.

A poster hanging in the living room shows a child with blonde pigtails holding, like at a rally, a sign in her hands that reads: "Teehee, I live in a solid house. And you???" (three question marks, yes). Hanging from a nail in the office is an old annual calendar of the Town & Country company. It shows a photograph of two monkeys and above it we read the "Town & Country motto for the year 2010," a passage from Schopenhauer: "The task is not so much to see what no one yet has seen, but to think what nobody yet has thought about that which everybody sees." What does this mean for Flair 113? "Fantastic"? What are Town & Country and the house with a name ending in the unlucky number 13 ultimately really about?

The manufacturer of the house, the franchise chain Town & Country, which was founded by Jürgen Dawo in 1997, is by now one of the most successful brand home manufacturers in Germany.[4] By 2013 the company had built about 21,000 homes, including close to 6,400 of the Flair series. Flair 113 was designed for a clientele which has a "great need for security but little equity," as economic expert Harald Willenbrock writes in his analysis of the company: "Dawo's credo is 'Cheaper than the good ones and safer than all others.'"[5] The company had half a billion euros in revenue in 2012 alone. Its designs, which are created in the company's headquarters in Thüringen, are "midway between houses that are beautiful but unaffordable and houses that are cheap, but that no one wants to live in, because they are ugly."[6] A base version Flair 113 costs 117,000 euros; the architect Katja Knüppel, one of six construction planners who design the various types of houses at the company headquarters, explained that the Flair 113 house looks "precisely the way most people imagine a house"; it is "an archetype."[7] Jürgen Dawo similarly states that the success of the house can be attributed to its "archaic form."[8] The company also offers Bauhaus boxes, but "we sold a mere four of those last year. Still, they are important for our image."[9]

Another reason for the success of Flair 113 is its pseudo individuality: just as in car manufacturing, the manufacturer deals with a manageable number of components that to the client appear as a wide selection of thirty house models and several hundred versions. Cost-cutting involves details: the homes are delivered with unpainted interior walls and without flooring, the 3,500-euro frost-protection barrier is dispensed with (instead the foundation is simply protected through gravel), and windows, staircases, and components are purchased in bulk, thus lowering the price.[10]

This is another reason for the aesthetic desolation of the suburbs. Bulk buying allows for discounts that small competitors cannot match. Jürgen Dawo sees this in pragmatically positive terms, referring to a trend toward the "Walmaritization" of the construction industry. "The account costing alone of the myriad funding options and energy-saving requirements of the Kreditanstalt für Wiederaufbau [Credit Institute for Reconstruction], which clients and the government nowadays demand, simply kills small providers." While a single energy-saving upgrade intended to meet future insulating standards would increase the price of a Flair 113 by about 60,000 euros, his engineers are working on solutions that, not least because of the mass production of houses, are to cost just 10,000 euros.[11]

This matters to Dawo's clients: by his reckoning eight million households are so-called threshold households that can just about afford a very cheap house.[12] These are people who otherwise live in the city in rental apartments or condos. They are his target group, they are the ones he wants to move from the city into his houses. This process is very much about "eliminating fear," Dawo explains, saying there is also a need to be a "psychiatrist."[13] This is why his salespeople distribute key chains shaped like safety pins; it is why they zero in on the clients' fears of the building contractor going bankrupt, of skyrocketing costs, of the mad architect who knowingly misleads the client about the cost of his design.

Dawo knows that there is a need for safety behind the desire for a house of one's own. "It is not surprising therefore that the company had the highest volume of sales ever in the midst of the financial crisis."[14]

In the construction industry the most money can be made with the less affluent. It has always been like that: in nineteenth-century Paris the highest rental yields were generated in the poorest arrondissements, because net rents were higher there in relation to the market value of the houses, whereas the residents of more upscale neighborhoods expected expensive decorations and better service.[15]

The drab, cheap houses in the countryside are attractive most of all because of the profit opportunities for the provider.

"But if the owners just happen to like these houses the way they are" goes a popular counterargument against the aesthetically motivated complaints that are raised in the name of good taste and aesthetics by architects and critics: after all, not everyone has to want to live like Palladio or Mies van der Rohe!

The argument sounds irrefutable, yet the scandal lies elsewhere: in the fact that the lobbies of the turnkey-ready have abolished any real choices and, as a result, the client's freedom as well, because the "free planning" that is technically offered is too expensive for most. Hardly anyone who builds one of those depressing cheap boxes in the countryside will say: I find the Villa Malcontenta kooky and ugly; I deliberately opted for these plastic windows and these strangely angular, purportedly designer-made door handles. The truth of the suburban misery lies in the fact that people dealing with a job and children do not have the time and the brass neck to contradict their solid-house builders and look for a carpenter to get a counteroffer for the plastic windows being provided. They do not know where to get the beautiful forms they have seen elsewhere. The supplier of the turnkey-ready box won't tell them: a construction industry that makes good money off these boxes that are thrown up in record time has no interest whatsoever in pointing out other options. It is a mistake to deplore the alleged lack of taste of suburbanites; the truth is that all action alternatives have been taken from them by the building lobbies—and the municipalities stand by and do nothing. Many people who buy a property requiring them to use a particular construction company feel they have no real power vis-à-vis the latter's specifications; they feel they have to take what just happens to be on offer—extras get expensive. Socialism with its *plattenbau* ideology lives on in the mass production of solid houses. From the point of view of the solid-house industry this is good business: an engineer whose solid-house construction company plonks sixty single-family homes a year in the countryside gets a commission from the cleaner and discounted prices from the plastic window manufacturer. If the client wants something else, the engineer has to redraw everything instead of just minimally modifying a basic design stored in the computer. He has to inquire about other windows, order other flooring, and find manufacturers and suppliers with whom he has not made any agreements regarding commissions. All of this not only creates more work for the engineer, but also cuts his profits. It follows from this that carpentry shops that manufacture windows and other traditional trades are pushed out of the market. The economic atrophy that turns city centers into wasteland has its counterpart outside the city in the serial houses that are individualized with home improvement center tinsel and whose appearance is determined by the pressure groups of the construction industry.

In return, clients are led to believe they have a number of options through a catalog of pseudo liberties: they can decorate the invariable pointed roof or half-hip-roof box "according to their wishes."

Unlike in traditional small towns in America, where a wide variety of types of houses are all built from the same material—usually wood—and with the same roofing material—slate—thus creating a homogenous townscape, European suburban developments are characterized by the terror of optical dissociation: one person chooses blue roof tiles, another favors black ones; one opts for a silver-colored metal door with triangular frosted-glass panes, another for the green door with yellow frame; one finds the look of his house boring and paints a red racing stripe on the façade, like the ones people used to put on small cars to make them look faster—and perhaps these attempts at individualization are also just indicators of unhappiness with the standardized whole.

American small town

Development area in Berlin

An odd paradox can be observed in the relationship between city and countryside: whereas in the countryside architecture is increasingly standardized and solid-house builders produce one single-family home after another like eggs in a laying battery, as the industrialization and serialization of suburban architecture progresses, massive ruralization can be observed in the city centers. A rural aesthetic of the unwrought, the authentic, and the hand-sawn is spreading in the centers.

Countermovements
The ruralization of urban centers

How much longer can a city that is increasingly shaped by tourists and an affluent, homogenous group of older newcomers, as well as by the upscale cafés and shops that were established to cater to them, remain a promise? How much longer can the big city function as a promise of a different way of life?

It seems that the more synthetic the appearance of city centers, the stronger the desire in the new metropolitan social circles for a rurally authentic aesthetic. People no longer look for the modern, anonymous, cold, or open character of the city, but rather for the idyll that has gone haywire outside in the suburbs and the country-side. The area to the south of Torstrasse in central Berlin looks not like a big city but like a reservation of lost small-town life. Just a few minutes from the sterile world of the office buildings of Berlin's city center there is a plethora of cafés and stores with heavy, rough-wood tables in front of them and with the menu of the day written with chalk on slate. Waiters in coarse linen shirts serve ecological prod-ucts with gnarled names. In the rural, idyllic one-way-street thicket of Berlin's Mitte district, where traffic is already restricted to walk-ing speed, arugula is called by its old German name, *rauke*, and the way shops like The Barn are furnished makes you feel you are some-where in the middle of Wisconsin in 1923, causing you to startle because the music is coming from white boxes rather than a gramo-phone. The iPhone at the black cash register looks like it has been left after a visit by an extraterrestrial. Rural aesthetics can also be found in the gentrified neighborhoods of Brooklyn: countering the drabness of the city with beards and check shirts, a utopia of the earthy and hands-on is projected, one that is inevitably accompanied by a degree of mustiness. Young lawyers and graphic designers sup-ping hearty root soups from heavy iron pots look like carpenters and maids in the wooden barn of a Quaker village. Many of those belonging to this scene hardly ever leave their neighborhood any-more; their physical range of motion is even less than that of a real villager. The rituals of this rural bohemian scene from a homogenous middle-class background—the anemic mix of parsnip cream, check shirts, traffic-restricted one-way streets, timber tables, and potato soups—recall the rituals of the nobility at the court of Louis XVI, who in the *hameau*, Marie Antoinette's artificial farm in the park of Versailles Palace, reenacted with great dedication the rural life that outside, beyond the palace fence, was happening as miserable reality.

In Berlin after the fall of the wall, a young urban scene was drawn to the cheap ruins in the environs. There, grotesque tableaus could be witnessed when, on weekends, entire armies of gallerists, software specialists, and small-press publishers wearing white pants and carrying bulging plastic bags from the delicatessen department of Kaufhaus des Westens descended upon the cheap ruins of East German farmhouses, savoring the romantic authenticity of ribbon villages, while outside, village youths plagued by unemployment and hemorrhage were slashing the tires of the old Range Rover. Next, monstrous agricultural machines would show up beyond the purportedly original stone walls to spray the endless fields with insecticides, bringing to mind that the countryside is in reality a hyper-industrialized zone rather than an idyll. Altercations with remaining villagers ensued; parties became ever scarcer, and eventually the summerhouse seekers retreated and moved their experiment in self-ruralization back into the city centers.

In the United States, sociologists have identified a more persistent countermovement of people who restore deteriorating small towns in upstate New York and rekindle life as an actual rural idyll that two generations earlier happened only in what is called the Village in Manhattan. As American author Ralph Martin notes: "Manhattan has long quit being cool and in Brooklyn rents are rising to the point where it now attracts only 'trustafarians'—children from extremely wealthy families who disguise themselves here as bohemians. Artists, writers, and authors—that is, the kind of people whose visible presence causes a place to become 'cool'—have for the most part moved to upstate New York or Maine, including, for instance, a large share of *New Yorker* writers." This ruralization of the bohemian scene is "a shock for all those who grew up dreaming of a wild metropolitan life: it almost seems as if the generation born around 1970 is the last one to which a life in New York, Paris, or London was a glittering promise."[16]

Many younger city dwellers who can afford to do so leave Manhattan and Brooklyn and venture on restoring small towns in the Hudson River Valley, where one can still find dilapidated classic American homes of the nineteenth and early twentieth centuries to snap up and renovate. The streets in towns like Hudson and Beacon are nowadays dominated by young urbanites who are putting their concept of a neo-rural idyll into practice. *The New York Times* has coined the term "NoBro" (North of Brooklyn) for this Brooklynization of the Hudson River Valley.[17] Interestingly, the dream living environment of the young creative folks who flock here, primarily from Brooklyn, and occupy entire towns and that of a conservative older population who are antiurbanist for different reasons seem to coincide in one curious point: the abundance of home-carpentered, home-baked, handmade, and locally harvested goods that one gets to see and buy in the new ideal towns of tattooed rural bohemians—the aesthetics of the local, the entire evocation of a world that can do without standardization and mass production, which is staged here by a younger avant-garde—has a surprising counterpart in the nostalgic pop-up towns of New Urbanism, most notably Celebration, the town built in Florida by The Walt Disney Company (see page 189ff.).

Worlds without an outside
The architecture of the new consciousness industries

> *"You were here before you entered this place,*
> *and you will still be here after you leave."*
> – Denis Diderot

In the twentieth century the high-rise was the visible symbol of economic power. Walter P. Chrysler, the industrialist and owner of the third-largest car manufacturer in the US, memorialized himself in 1930 by putting up a building in the midst of Manhattan that rose above the urban canyons like a wild exclamation mark and was obviously meant as a warning to competitors and doubters. At the time of its completion the 1,046-foot-tall Chrysler Building was the world's tallest building. Nowadays, built symbols look different. The major high-rise projects of our time, such as New York's One World Trade Center, appear, if anything, like tragic farewells to a building type. With its twisted shape and almost 200-foot-tall, glass-clad concrete base, it is an architecture of trauma; everything about its form bespeaks a fear of attacks.

The new architectural symbols of power are going up in California—and they look different, if one can still speak of a "look." On a site in Cupertino measuring 2.15 million square feet, Norman Foster is building a massive glass donut for Apple, a merely four-story, ring-shaped structure in which 12,000 people—the population of a small town—are supposed to work. An artificial jungle will be created in the empty center of the complex. The building itself will barely be visible from the street, as it is located in a large park. Given the structure's dimensions, one cannot really refer to it as a building; just as the largest Minoan palace of Knossos in antiquity, which had a built surface area of almost 250,000 square feet, was more like a small town, the headquarters being built by Apple can be better grasped in urbanist rather than in architectural terms. The world being created here is one that people can and must stay in the whole day—a self-contained sphere.

Meanwhile, Frank O. Gehry has also designed a gigantic annex building, for the corporate headquarters of Facebook, located just a half-hour drive from Cupertino. In Menlo Park, near San Francisco Bay, a one-story office block with 430,000 square feet of surface area will serve as the largest open-plan office in the world, explains Facebook founder Mark Zuckerberg. The roof of the vast space will be a park with trees; from the outside it will look like a landscape. And underneath, in the open-plan office, the sheer size of the structure will also create the impression of an artificial landscape that is dotted with cabin-like meeting rooms resembling small villages in a prairie full of peacefully grazing desks. The world's most powerful companies no longer produce towers but working landscapes—after the strong-form statement of the tower come weak-form buildings, buildings that are intentionally formless.

What does this mean? Both buildings are located in America, where the landscape has its own symbolic history. Nineteenth-century American mythology was shaped by the pioneers' trek west; its narrative was horizontal expansion: the building of the railroad, the conquest of the landscape. In the twentieth century this horizontal expansion was followed by the adventure of the vertical: early twentieth-century America invented the skyscraper, and the American hero of the twentieth century was the cowboy of the vertical, the astronaut. With Apple and Facebook, a pioneer aesthetic returns: employees roam through gardens, parks, and jungles—it is almost as if the arrival of the nineteenth-century pioneers in the virgin forests of the West Coast is being reenacted.

Apple Headquarters, Cupertino (Norman Foster)
Facebook Headquarters, Menlo Park (Frank O. Gehry)

If we regard Apple und Facebook as commercial consciousness machines that analyze and control our thoughts and actions, then we can see a nice ideological punchline in the way their corporate headquarters are rendered invisible: Facebook confronts us like a friendly force of nature, like a transformation of "history into nature," as Roland Barthes once wrote. The social network becomes a natural part of our ecosystem, with the power and the operating systems disappearing underground. Just as the villain's headquarters in early James Bond movies are located beneath rocks, power disguises itself as nature and the work in it as play.

A company that privacy groups have exposed as a sinister, multi-tentacled, information-devouring monster clads itself here in the most cheerful kindergarten costume. The people in their nice landscape, so the message goes, just want to play. The New York-based architecture critic William Hanley speaks of a "corporate kindergarten" in view of the skateboarding courses and computer game corners with which Facebook is trying to make the workplace in Menlo Park attractive for young businessmen and programmers. Looked at in this light, the cheerfully, if not childishly, swinging architecture may be an equivalent to the type of harmless, childlike hacker/whistleblower/super-programmer nerd whose Edward Snowden-like milky bland physiognomy stands in sharp contrast to the global devastation caused by his actions: a house designed for the cute, evil monster child that reprograms the world from the children's room, hacking the living daylights out of it.

The Facebook headquarters and Apple's glass spaceship, along with its enclosed Garden of Eden, can also be seen as claustrophobic. Both invent worlds that no longer have an outside, as they counter, with immersion, the pathos of the panoramic view of the world that the high-rise offered on its executive floor. People go out (Apple) or up (Facebook) into the garden and at the same time move further into the artificial world. The new gardens of the major corporations also have something of what the literary scholar Robert Pogue Harrison calls the "perverse beauty" of the gardens of Versailles, which delighted the power elite of their time with, among other things, a recreated farmstead and a jungle-like adventure forest in which a cheerful version of pre-civilizational life was reenacted.

Corporations are deliberately moving into green surroundings with their headquarters: inventing a second nature, a working landscape in the place of the city. What is the meaning of the aesthetics of disappearance, the culture of the weak form, which characterized the Facebook headquarters in particular, but also the Apple building, whose form and dimensions are impossible to make out from street level? Shortly before its new administration spaceship, Apple introduced the so-called iCloud: information is saved externally, in a virtual "cloud" from which it can be retrieved on any Apple device. Calling this virtual power center "cloud" was almost like charging it with religious meaning and making the technical process appear like a force of nature.

The cloud, which sends memories to people the way Zeus sent his lightning bolts, is perhaps the most powerful symbol of a decade of invisibility that began in 2001—the year when the attack on the towers of the World Trade Center brought with it constant alarm about ever-present yet invisible danger. The terror of the invisible had its parallel in the financial markets, where seemingly safe material values turned out to be fictitious. And finally, the invisible radiation in Fukushima destroyed the belief in nuclear power. During this time of continuously alarming, invisible phenomena, Apple became one of the world's most valuable companies with its promise of positive dematerialization. The iPhone is replacing the record shelves, the record player, the map, the navigation system, the phone book, the calendar, the camera: all these objects have disappeared from everyday life. With its "iCloud" the company provided the signet for the dematerialization of the perceptible: today the cloud is what the high-rise used to be—a symbol of an era and at the same time the seat of real power. The aesthetics of invisibility that characterizes the new corporate headquarters in California may reflect these developments. As autonomous worlds, they replace the city outside with cheerful simulacra: here, too, there are "squares" and "cafés" and all the furnishings of old cities, except that access is tightly controlled. These worlds, too, are versions of a new Versailles.

The home spies on its occupants
Hudson Yards

In Manhattan, the Hudson Yards urban development project is currently under construction. It will ultimately include seventeen buildings with apartments, offices, and a shopping center: with a total of 17 million square feet of commercial and residential space it will be a city within a city. Hudson Yards is a fortress against the uncertainties of a metropolis, the developers say. A 13.2-megawatt cogeneration system will be able to keep up the power supply even in the event of a total blackout, such as after Hurricane Sandy—under such circumstances the Yards could become a refuge for its neighbors as well.

In addition to an ecologically advanced energy supply system, residents will be able to control lighting, temperature, and household appliances via their smartphones. "Thousands of sensors in combination with anonymously collected data will quantify the residents' behavior, from shopping habits to energy use," thus allowing the operators to optimize their quality of life in terms of fresh air inside the house, noise generation, and energy consumption.

New York, Hudson Yards

Obviously, what is celebrated here as a technological innovation that primarily increases comfort and saves energy also spells something else for the future of housing: the home controlling its occupants, registering their every movement. When is the fridge opened? What is taken out? When is the computer being used and what is being googled when? When are the windows opened, and how many people are in which rooms at what times? Theoretically, the home today is already better at spying on its occupants than any spying technology from outside with directional microphones.

Until now, big data in urban planning was important mainly in optimizing traffic flows, avoiding congestion, and reducing empty cab runs. The observation and prediction of human behavior in space, usually in cities—which is something that MIT's SENSEable City Lab, among others, is concerned with—is by now used to control tourism as well. A new form of data-driven city planning is being developed. The World's Eyes project uses the pictures that tourists put online to study how people travel and experience a city; what they find worthy of being photographed and what places they have not yet reached in droves; what regions are "still free from the tourist buzz," and to what extent attractions such as artworks or spectacular buildings channel tourists into unattractive areas; and in what way this influx affects sales figures and demography.

The next step as part of this bottom-up monitoring, which involves assessing digital traces left by residents, rather than spying from the outside, is the analysis of data generated by sensors and devices inside the home—the interpretation of the digital shadow a resident leaves on his own four walls.

Eventually, it may happen that people who do not want the operator of a residential complex to collect data that is supposedly intended merely to increase comfort and ecological efficiency will arouse suspicion—by not wanting the system to register when they come and go, even though it would allow the heat and lighting in their home to be controlled much more efficiently and bring down heating costs for the complex as a whole. This will give rise to as yet greatly underestimated conflicts concerning the very essence of privacy.

On the path toward the transparent citizen—about whom commercial providers already have so much information that they can control a person's desires and behavior—a home that can readily generate movement profiles is a potentially significant informant. The "smart home" could create a comprehensive picture of the personalities of its users, and it is just a matter of time before industry, insurance companies, and the police try to get their hands on the personal data of residential complexes such as Hudson Yards. The fact that data collection—by means of various devices, sensors in the car, and soon at an increased level in the home as well—has so far met with relatively little public outrage, compared with the 1983 census in Germany and in spite of the NSA scandal, may also be due to a changed cultural climate in a society whose priorities have shifted from freedom and personal responsibility to comfort and safety.

What possible alternatives are there to these scenarios? In order to understand what future habitation could look like beyond such luxury dystopias, we must take a closer look at the history of housing.

Bailey House, Case Study House No. 21, Los Angeles (Pierre Koenig)

Chapter 2

Being at Home

A Brief Phenomenology of Habitation

A house is a built psychogram. The history of civic housing is a history not just of self-projection, but also of efforts at self-discovery: the home is supposed to express something, tell something about oneself. Souvenirs turned the living room into a museum of one's own past; period furniture brought the resident closer to aristocracy. In a long-inhabited home, the lived life sediments like annual rings: the stacked, scratched, yellowed things tell the story of the occupants. In a newly occupied home, furniture, pictures, and wall colors are part of a design: this is what life should look like.

Few things reveal as much about a society as the ways in which its members furnish their homes. For this reason alone it is interesting to see what home-related needs are met—or, indeed, aroused in the first place—by furniture makers and interior design magazines. What are the forms with which they respond to social movements and moods? What characterizes the home today? What forms do home life and its shell take and why?

Farnsworth House, near Plano, Illinois
(Mies van der Rohe)

Elements of architecture

The window

The history of modern architecture is also a history of window enlargement. As a result of the reinforced concrete technology developed by Auguste Perret and Le Corbusier, which made it possible to build a house like a shelf made of concrete, the façade lost its supporting function. It was replaced by the curtain wall, which could be made entirely of glass. The view from the home changed abruptly. Le Corbusier's Villa Savoye near Paris, which was built in 1929—the same year when Luis Buñuel shot his film *Un chien andalou* with the famous scene of a razor slicing through an eye—replaced the vertical window with ribbon windows. The view of the landscape now suggested a film running before the eyes of the resident. The window, etymologically a "wind eye" in a stone wall, had grown and ran across the wall like an incision.

The exterior walls of Mies van der Rohe's 1951 Farnsworth House in Illinois ended up being made of glass. The house, once raised by piling up stones to provide protection, was now but a roof; the protective wall had become invisible. It felt like being right in the middle of nature. The entire wall was now an eye outward rather than immersion, protection; a view out into the world, an eye without lids and lashes, without muntins, blinds, or roof overhang.

The skeptical world: the shrinking window.   By now, a reverse process can be observed in various areas: windows are shrinking again. The reasons for this contraction process vary.

The modern desire for the house to open up to the world and ultimately merge with the outside, which played an aesthetic game with the enlargement of the window into a transparent glass wall, was from the outset countered by a skeptical Modernism describing the view from the window as a portal to a world of fictions and nonactualities. Lurking outside of the cave, in the outdoors, is not the real world casting its shadow into the cave but rather a shadow world itself. The most famous story of this kind is E.T.A. Hoffmann's *The Sandman*, in which the student Nathanael looks through a window into the room of the beautiful Olimpia and falls for her, until he is forced to realize that she is but a human-like automaton with dead eyes. What looks in as a promise is an illusion, whereas the real—in this case his beloved, Clara—is that which is inside.

This alienation from the outside would subsequently become a defining element of many modernist forms of habitation. Paradoxically, it was at odds with the aesthetics of dissolving boundaries that characterized architectural High Modernism. Everything is centered inward, like in a spaceship shielding its occupants from an outside world that is hostile to life. Immersion, isolation is the desired ideal state, which as early as the 1960s led to what Richard Sennett has described as the "tyranny of intimacy."[18]

Windowless bliss: the reactor of the private. Even so, many actual suburban homes of the 1960s featured at least one picture window accommodating the modern penchant toward the visual dissolution of the wall. Contemporary solid prefab houses, on the other hand, reduce the window area to an absolute minimum.

While radical cost saving and ecologically motivated energy conservation regulations have prompted this contraction, other reductions of window area are aesthetically motivated: the architects who designed the Delbrück building at Potsdamer Platz in Berlin reduced the windows to the size of shooting slits in order for the compact structure to appear higher from a distance, thus relying on a trompe l'oeil effect.

Viewless buildings: the US Embassy as an architecture of panic
Opened in 2008, the American Embassy in Berlin may go down in the history of architecture as a typical building of the 2000s. What this embassy conveys is, in essence, a combination of security hysterics and nostalgia. It looks like a knight's castle that can be pieced together at a home improvement store. With windows narrowed down to slits and a fortified tower of sorts that is missing only one thing, battlements, it appears as if it had been originally planned for a different and rougher part of the world. We should be fair: of course, an embassy needs to be secured, but except for bunkers and centers for pesticide testing, there are few other modern buildings

that present themselves so shuttered toward the street as this embassy. If a house could stand with its arms crossed it would look like this. Such crossbars are used to armor the headlights and windshields of military and water cannon vehicles. This kind of armoring is used when there is a need to look out but not let anything in. The upper part of the façade facing Behrenstrasse has no windows at all; here, the United States presents itself as an utterly impenetrable, erratic bunker object.

left: US Embassy, Berlin (Moore Ruble Yudell)
middle: Delbrück Haus, Berlin (Kollhoff Architekten)
right: Single-family home in Kladow, near Berlin

As it turned out this was, in fact, the part of the building where the wiretapping experts of the NSA had their offices, and the architecture made no particular effort to hide the secretiveness.

Despite, or perhaps because of, the fact that it is geared toward the threat of an attack, because of its obsessive armoring against a menacing Other, this building is typical of the city of today: public space, which had once seemed a promise, is now perceived to be a threat. The American Embassy is not the image of a country that once was a promise to immigrants from around the world, a place for new beginnings and self-projections: the embassy is the emblem of a country traumatized by 9/11 and the impact of globalization.

The building is not unique in its new windowlessness: the Freedom Tower in New York, built to replace the World Trade Center and now the most prominent self-portrait of the United States after

September 11, 2001, sits atop a 200-foot-tall windowless concrete base. A safety precaution, the explanation goes, otherwise terrorists could topple the tower with a truckload of explosives. Two hundred feet of pure reinforced concrete. Glazing mitigates the bunker-like effect at the World Trade Center, but it is a trompe l'oeil, a mirror hiding an impenetrable wall. A metaphor for transparency and democracy in the history of twentieth-century architecture, glass here mutates into a fortifying coating that reflects everything approaching it.

If we can trust the images produced by the architecture of a period, if the 1950s and 1960s were thus decades of absolute transparency, of elegant glass houses—Lever House, the Seagram Building, the Case Study Houses—then the years after 2001 are the years of great window- and viewless-ness.

In other cases the reasons for window contraction are more complex and this is nowhere more evident than in the design history of the object occupying the garage, that utterly windowless house to the side of the house: the automobile.

A view of the garage
What automotive design reveals

Even those who do not care about automoblies should be interested in automotive design. For nowhere else is so such much money invested in psychological warfare through forms, and nowhere else are so many market researchers, psychologists, and designers working on recognizing the merest shifts in the psychosocial fabric. No other industry is putting so much effort into trying to sell a product that does not really need to be replaced every three years. The pressure to seduce specifically through aesthetics is growing in view of the technological convergence among competitors. This is yet another reason why automotive design is such a sensitive indicator of social changes.

So what does the design of cars today tell us? This field, too, is dominated by two form genres, two symptoms: nostalgia and hysterics. On the one hand, retro fashion, the evocation of the cars the affluent baby boomer generation used to have as toy cars: the Ford Mustang, the Chevrolet Camaro, the Fiat 500, or the Mini. When not escaping into the past, design shows a different escapist tendency that is already prevalent in architecture: isolation from the outside world. One of the most conspicuous changes in car design, too, concerns window sizes.

In a 1963 Mercedes 230 SL the driver sat as if within a vitrine. Since then the windows have been shrinking from year to year, and those we have nowadays resemble shooting slits of sorts that are cut into the sheet-metal fortress to retain an essential measure of overview. What is the reason behind this diminution of windows? One is the stability of the vehicle. Anyone driving a Citroën DS—to which Roland Barthes devoted his most famous essay— would die if the car overturned. This was even truer of high-performance convertibles such as the Ferrari California Spider, in which Alain Delon showed himself in 1964. Anyone buying this car was not thinking of possible accidents, but rather of acceleration, of an open life, of the best-case scenario.

Mercedes 230 SL (1963)
Mercedes A 200 (2014)

Thinking of life from the perspective of death

SUVs, those heavy passenger cars derived from pickup trucks that displaced the convertible as ideal showpiece vehicles in the world of dream cars, do not cater to such a need: the driver and passengers disappear behind dark-tinted glass. Isolation against a hostile outside world, rather than opening, is the dominant design theme. Some carmakers try to counter the sense of claustrophobia by glazing the roof, which entails a bizarre perceptual shift: the road and the driving public are blocked out as much as possible and the car takes on the form of a vessel that is open only at the top.

Even convertibles are different. They are, like so much else these days, conceived from the perspective of death: rather than possible happiness, their formal language bespeaks the threat of an accident, of failure, of the worst-case scenario. Safety dominates everything. The Mini Roadster is supposed to be fun, indeed, but in the event it overturns, two chrome-plated roll bars stand at attention behind the headrests; gleaming chrome reminders, anxiety humps, ever-present sculptures of fear.

The demand for safety leads to strange visual effects. Some car-makers offer a so-called night-vision system. An infrared camera films the roadway at night and the image is displayed on the wind-shield. Drivers now have a choice: they can either try to look with their own eyes for what pops up in the dark, or they can focus on the film, which shows a lot more. The windshield, the window on reality, becomes a screen on which a movie is projected that presents reality as a surreal image. While driving, you watch a movie of real life, and the driver's experience is much like that of poor Nathanael in Hoff-mann's *The Sandman*: he looks out of the window and cannot tell whether what he believes he is seeing is real or a dangerous illusion.

The front sections of present-day cars, too, seem to project a hys-terization, a transition from a society focusing on freedom and promise to one restricting itself to the promise of the greatest pos-sible safety. While the glass panes shrink to the point that cars look like they are squinting, the front sections are turning into masks of a Greek tragedy. We see visages distorted with fear, seized with panic, radiator mouths opened wide, headlights in the shape of glaring anger wrinkles, and barred metal jaws, as if the car were feeding on whole hoofed animals rather than gas. Armed with light and chrome teeth, the radiator jaws communicate that the driver considers pub-lic space a place that is about eating and being eaten.

While the car's exterior thus displays a kind of turbo-bellicose hypermobility, its interior is, by contrast, increasingly turning into a piece of real estate that radiates a homey duskiness. Where thin steering wheels, scrawny gearshifts, cold imitation leather, and lots of metal used to reflect the desired ideal of the commanding, active machinist, the interior of today's cars is dominated by an atmosphere of radical comfort and coziness that is strangely contrary to the belligerent exterior: plush seats, a thousand buttons, little lights, wood veneer—the same crowded coziness reigns that we are familiar with from living rooms. Once the symbol of new departure, of escaping immobilized circumstances, the car now always carries the living room with it.

Metamorphoses of the storage room: the garage as a market square. In the United States, a more pleasing repurposing of the car storage room is the so-called garage sale, an event unfamiliar to Europeans, at which the garages and driveways of the—socially speaking—largely quiet suburbs turn into public flea markets for a few hours. In his book *Magical Urbanism*, Mike Davis describes how particularly Latin-American immigrants taking up residence in dilapidated suburban homes perpetuate this institution of the garage sale. They set up workshops and small stores in the garages of suburban residences, thereby returning the vibrant, dense, small-town small-trade structure to the cities that had lost it due to their modern suburbanization. Thus the house without windows, of all places, is becoming the breeding ground for a new architecture of encounter.

The wall

Most houses in European suburbs are constructed from artificially produced sandstone blocks and plastered—more recently with added thermal insulation. When tapping on interior walls, you feel that they are papier-mâché-like drywalls. With the insulated new-construction homes outside the city, the sense of what a house is changes: for centuries, the brick wall embodied the solid and the glass pane the fragile. Children were admonished to kick the soccer ball only against the wall and not in the direction of the living room window. Today, the reverse is true: modern safety glass withstands an SUV backing up into it, whereas the insulated composite wall panel disintegrates into its unsightly components even when merely shot at with normal soccer balls. Modern psychology still has to analyze what it means for people's sense of security and comfort when the haptic sense and the sense of the reliability of things are duped in this way.

Nowadays, climate protection is a mantra of construction ideology that only needs to be recited for the most absurd things to become possible. Ever more pervasive domestic technology is required to elaborately ensure climate control when, as a power guzzler, the technology itself negatively influences the climate. Thermal insulation composite systems, too, are a product of ideology and fashions rather than the result of ecological rethinking. Having been around since the 1950s, they are a product of the least ecological period in the history of mankind. In Germany, a thermal insulation composite system was used in a building for the first time in Berlin in 1957, that is, around the same time when hermetically sealed cheese started to appear in stores and when the US company Swanson flooded the market with nonperishable three-part TV dinners whose food-to-packaging ratio reached new records of inefficiency.

The ingredients of the house sealed with a thermal insulation composite system are no less unecological: in order to protect the environment, entire oil fields are turned into rigid polystyrene foam, extruded polystyrene foam, or rigid polyurethane foam at huge cost. It is synthetic material that is supposed to ensure ecological correctness as insulation material behind the plaster. Complete thermal insulation, which aims to save the climate, is thus part of the global energy problem that it is supposed to solve even in its production. And this is ignored with a stubbornness that hides other, purely commercial interests.

The economization of form: insulation mania. In the debate regarding complete thermal insulation it is worth once in while looking at things from the so-called tradesman's perspective. Building a conventional brick wall costs time and money. For the general contractor, constructing a house using thermal insulation composite system technology involves much greater profit margins. If you have ever seen the speed at which a few masons with suitcase-size industrial stones build a wall and at what speed insulation panels are subsequently bolted or glued onto this wall (indeed, glued, with best wishes to climate protection activists), before a bunch of plasterers armed with spray guns puts a finishing coat on it within a few hours—if you have seen that a complete house is built in about a fifth of the time in this way and still ends up costing almost as much as a classic brick building—then you also understand why houses are now almost exclusively built this way. Because this is how solid house construction companies make the greatest profits. The ecological aspect merely serves to cloak an economic advantage: more than anything, complete thermal insulation puts more money in the pockets of the building contractors.

"Sustainable" it is not, that's for sure. We can be reasonably confident that in ten years' time the insulated world of new construction homes will be a hazardous waste depot in the shape of a house, not least because much of it has not been mounted in a technically correct manner: the polystyrene panels bow; water condensates between the insulation and the exterior wall plaster, without being able to completely evaporate; the plaster cracks; the insulation material is gradually soaked; and ten years later everything will come down.

Until recently, walls were among the few things that you could not and did not need to throw away; complete thermal insulation changes this. For the insulation industry this is good business: every ten to twenty years it receives the order to reinsulate the same house. It is almost like a commercial perpetual motion machine.

Alternatives: the future of the wall. What can a wall still be? What, exactly, is a wall anyway? The answer seems mundane: a wall is a panel in a space. Sometimes it has openings in it that are called door or window. The German word for "wall," *wand*, derives from the Old High German *uonedh*, which means a mesh covered with mud. This is interesting: contrary to what we think today, the wall used to be a textile object, a mesh, a fabric. This is also suggested by the etymological affinity of *wand* with the word *gewand*, which means "garment," as well as by the word "tabernacle," meaning "tent," for the small cupboard that holds the host in Christian churches. The architect Gottfried Semper referred to "man's second skin," and in the more recent past, numerous architects have tried to build structures with textile walls. Shigeru Ban's Curtain Wall House is one case in point, Petra Blaisse's curtain-framed room in

Rem Koolhaas's Maison à Floriac near Bordeaux and Toyo Ito's 1985 Pao for the Tokyo Nomad Girl are two others.

In each of these cases the living space is mobile, flexible, rather than static, and adapts itself to its environment: a structure halfway between a house and a tent. Not everyone is able to live like this, but the concept of the wall as a flexible, textile zone rather than a static panel leads to amazing solutions even in the renovation of *plattenbau* buildings and social housing from the 1950s to the 1980s.

Proposals for countering the insulation mafia: a wall of glass and fabric. In Paris, the architects Anne Lacaton, Frédéric Druot, and Jean-Philippe Vassal rebuilt a derelict social housing project, the Tour Bois-le-Prêtre in the 17th arrondissement, that was built in 1959 based on designs by Raymond Lopez. This 165-foot-high residential tower with sixteen floors and almost one hundred apartments had been renovated in the 1980s by installing eternit panels in a depressing bicolor look and PVC windows. After this first renovation the building really came to resemble the drab structures that, from the East European *plattenbau* projects to the French HLM slums, lie around large European cities like a gloomy concrete belt. Eventually, the decision was made to demolish the tower. The state demolition program provided 15,000 euros for the demolition of an old apartment and about 150,000 euros for the new construction of

Curtain Wall House,
Itabashi (Shigeru Ban)

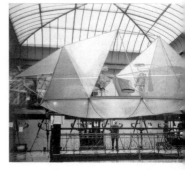

Nomad Girl's House,
Tokyo (Toyo Ito)

a housing unit. The architect Anne Lacaton, along with her partners Frédéric Druot and Jean-Philippe Vassal, suggested a different option. The firm familiarized itself with low-cost housing and the use of greenhouse walls. In the north of Paris they were able to radically remodel several apartments for the same amount by taking down the old façade elements and placing a construction with spacious, glazed winter gardens for each apartment like a shelf in front of it.

Tour Bois-le-Prêtre, Paris
(Anne Lacaton, Frédéric Druot,
Jean-Philippe Vassal)

In place of the old, depressingly small windows offering a view into the distance, the residents now have the effect of a modernist luxury apartment awash with light thanks to a large glass façade. When it rains, the children can play in the sheltered winter gardens, which also provide space to create a small garden. Each apartment grows in size by about 235 to 420 square feet as a result of the exterior living area—even suburban row houses do not offer much more green area. Rents remain unchanged, energy costs were reduced by the insulating effect, and in their own way the architects restore the old promise of Modernism: light, air, and sun instead of a den with a peephole. Social housing was thus turned into a building with a new, open entrance area that is reminiscent, if anything, of the luxury apartment buildings along the beaches of Rio de Janeiro. The ground floor now has a kindergarten and communal spaces for language courses and tenant meetings. Having been abandoned by the rationalist reductive modernism of the banlieue towers, the culture of entering, of reception is once again celebrated: where people used to scurry in dim neon light between bars and mailboxes to the elevators, they now enter the building in what is like a stately hotel lobby.

The remodeling of the derelict tower is seminal especially from an energy-related point of view: after the renovation the energy use dropped from 17 to just 7.5 kilowatt hours per square foot annually. A comparable project the architects are currently planning in Bordeaux aims to reduce energy use from 13.4 to 1.8 kilowatt hours. Yet how are the winter gardens insulated, considering that the architects are installing mere thin-gauge polycarbonate elements like the ones familiar from greenhouses? What makes it possible are curtains by the French manufacturer Isotiss: made of aluminum foil, new wool, and fabric, they gleam like silver and serve as insulation at night.

The advantages of this winter-garden remodeling are obvious: it creates additional space that can take the place of a suburban yard, and so the tenants are kept in the city. The drab functional architecture with its slit-like windows is transformed into an amply glazed form that abounds in intervening spaces and façade plasticity, almost evoking loggias and the bow fronts of older buildings in its spatial effect. The hazardous waste problem of conventional thermal insulation—which even optimistic forecasts expect to crop up in a few decades when millions of cubic meters of insulation foam will need to be disposed of—is avoided. And finally, the winter gardens allow for natural ventilation in the summer, as the sliding elements of the façade can be opened. The curtains allow for the control of light incidence, temperature, and atmosphere on a scale between openness and protection. Which brings us back to the etymological roots of the wall, or *wand*, in the textile object, the *uonedh*.

Why is not a lot more postwar building stock renovated in the exact same way as the Tour Bois-le-Prêtre? This tower illustrates what can be done with seemingly unsalvageable postwar housing projects. It is both a social and an aesthetic model for the possible renovation of the suburbs—and an ecological alternative to complete thermal insulation that any building policies should take into consideration, including the German one which, most recently, has been dazzled not just by plaster and insulating foam.

And yet many contractors who print out "individual solutions" from their design computers do not accommodate wishes for a double-layer winter garden construction as built by Lacaton and Vassal. The houses they build still look the same as they did four hundred years ago, just uglier and, in comparison, poorly made: a stone wall, a hole for the door, a hole for the windows, a pitched roof. Progress—the house of the twenty-first century—is this box, only this time it has a polystyrene disguise and a couple of solar cells on the tile-roof cap.

The roof

The roof as we see it jutting out of the landscape by the thousands in the suburbs is another illustration of economic forces underlying established forms of construction. They are roofs of a kind that has been around for centuries—if you ignore what has been screwed onto them. Even previously idyllic Bavarian villages and charming farmsteads are having their red roofs half-tiled with mercilessly defacing solar panels. Why is there not an appropriate, nice-looking form of solar roof catching on in the construction of single-family homes? Why are people building houses the same way as five hundred years ago, only to subsequently bolt a photovoltaic system onto the tile roof?

This patchwork technique is partly due to design specifications of the relevant municipalities, which allow roofs to be only partly covered with solar cells, so as to preserve the townscape, which is defined by red roofs—even if this does not benefit the overall impression.[19] A deeper reason why technologically advanced solar tiles[20] are not used more often, or why roofs are not covered completely with solar cells in place of tiles, may once again be that it is not in the interest of a powerful construction industry. If convincing solar roofs that do without tiles were to prevail on a large scale, this would precipitate the decline of pressed clay roofing tiles, which already saw a drop from 881 million in 2001 to 631 million in 2009—hence the lobbying of the roof tile industry for the solar half-ass. But what happens underneath the roofs?

The rooms of the house
Residential utopias: between garage and living room

If furniture advertising not only reflects and caters to the domestic needs and ideals of its time, but often also stokes those needs and wants in the first place, then it will be interesting to subject the ideals and ideologies of habitation to "form criticism" by taking a look at the living rooms in the advertisements of different decades.

On the sofa
Over the decades the sofa has come to look more and more like a bed. On the sofa of 1961 it is still impossible to imagine any other than an upright sitting position, or a single sleeping person bent double.

1950s living room
1970s sofa

Advertising campaigns of the 1970s, on the other hand, feature kids jumping around and adults rolling over on sofas, while furniture makers cut up the classic sofa into cubes that could be pushed together to create bed landscapes.

Since the 1990s the hypertrophy of the sofa has reached ever new heights, indicating a mood change. The sofa of the 1970s was a jumping and lounging site covered with colorful patterns or warm corduroy fabrics for the relaxing family. The 1980s sofa competed against this hippiesque furniture style with formally austere, cold leather sofas whose ideal owner had to be imagined with his tie just loosened and a cocktail glass in front of New York-themed photographic wallpaper. The 1990s sofa was again different: the seating surface came to be as deep as a narrow double bed. If you didn't immediately lie down on it lengthwise, but rather, as is customary on a sofa, with your feet toward the coffee table, you were forced to adopt a semiprostrate position with legs stretched and neck bent, a position from which it was impossible to get up again. The lounge is a paradigmatic piece of furniture. Sinking into it, you duck away from the world and become immobilized. In the clubs and bars of the 1990s, where such furniture was also found, the windows were often replaced with aquariums, with the softly soporific music of French electropop bands bubbling in accompaniment: one was out of the world, under water. The lounge sofa (usually L-shaped to allow for one's exhausted feet to be up) was the iconic furniture of great fatigue, the platform of soft self-immersion. If you sank into it in a sitting/lying position you would not even make it to bed anymore, where you could have really rested.

Only in the 1960s was there a brief moment that seemed to herald the end of the sofa. The entire living room turned into a bed, albeit a sloped one, a dune of velvet, as built by the architect/utopian Claude Parent. Born in Neuilly in 1923, Parent rethought the living room more radically than anyone else in the last century. He planned a revolution of the living room, a destructive blow against the concept of furniture—and the idea for this came to him, fittingly, in a derelict bunker. Between 1942 and 1944 the German Wehrmacht had built roughly 8,200 bunkers along a 1,670-mile-long stretch of the European west coast to prevent a landing by allied forces. Many of these bunkers have since slid down the dunes after fierce winter storms and are now stuck in sand, tilted, slanted, as if dropped from a great height. One day in the 1960s, when Parent was touring these dune landscapes in his Jeep together with the philosopher Paul Virilio, who was nine years his junior, they stopped at a bunker that was half-buried in the soft sand and entered it through a narrow opening: "Inside, you tumbled through a strange room. The floor was so sloped that you couldn't tell whether what you were standing on was a slanted floor or a former wall." The concepts of "wall," "floor," "up," and "down" no longer made any sense at all. It was, Parent remembers, a sense of space that you couldn't have anywhere else: a delirium, a dizziness that even the most turbulent Baroque churches could not induce.[21] Since the visit to the bunker, the sensation of standing on an incline never let go of Parent. He began to deliberately bring things out of balance. He built a villa near Versailles for the industrialist Gaston Drusch that looked as if a Bauhaus cube had settled, quite similar to the Atlantic bunker, into the ground at a 45-degree angle—but things like this were already no longer extreme enough for him. He decided to build only sloped floors from then on. With Virilio he wrote pamphlets like "Vivre à l'Oblique" (Living on the Slope). And even today he speaks with undiminished enthusiasm about how this life on the slope could stimulate social relationships and steer them in new directions: "Consider how boring it is within our homes. The kid stays in the assigned kid's room while the grown-up sits on an inherited couch in another room. We're completely overfurnished. What would it be like, on the other hand, if space were understood more playfully, more freely, if movement and being in a space also could mean climbing, reclining, sliding?"[22] What would happen, Parent asked, if you made people group in ways different to those required by the given social parameters of "chair," "table," "sofa," "bed," etc? Can furnitureless architecture affect dynamics between people? Claude Parent explored this question, and in so doing became one of the most important social utopians in the modern history of architecture. The first icon of the "oblique" was a church. It opened in 1966 in Nevers. From the outside, it looked like a bunker and the floors were as sloping and slanted as the concrete ruins on the Atlantic. Parent turned the home into a paradox halfway house between cave and slope. At the 1970 Venice Biennale, he installed an artificial landscape of sloping surfaces in the French pavilion. He remodeled his own home, removing all furniture and instead building a landscape of ramps and slopes in the rooms. Immediately, the ancient discussion flared up again—one that had already distinguished the Dorians on Crete, who sat at the table, from the people of ancient Smyrna, who followed the Oriental example and ate while reclining—whether life is more desirable with chairs at the table or without.[23]

A photograph from the time shows Parent together with family and guests, with him sitting like a guru of furnitureless existence on one of those sloped surfaces and the others squatting and lying around him, like a deconstructivist remake of the School of Athens.

It was difficult to tell what was "wall" and what was "roof" and it was in this dissolution of categories and classification systems that Parent wanted to find new freedom. The house became a landscape again: people were lounging and rolling around the slope like a horde of gorillas. This was also a sociodynamic sign at a time when lying side by side or in disorder in public was still perceived as morally dubious. Parent's daughter Chloé writes: "I ran with my dog over ramps and let marbles roll down—my parents had banned all furniture from the house. There were hardly any doors. You lay on plateaus and in caverns … From the day the workmen came to install the ramps, the extraordinary became everyday life. It was exciting for me as a child. I no longer belonged to the bourgeois world, in which you inherited valuable period furniture from your ancestors and ate at tables surrounded by six tall chairs … We ate lying down at a small, flat table, which you could also lie under. In places soft spots had been embedded in the ramps that you couldn't see— visitors would often scream in terror when they stepped on such a spot."[24]

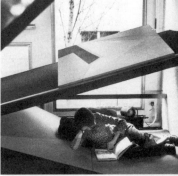

The world of Ikea is far removed from such residential utopias.[25] The 2014 Ikea catalog features living rooms that have no windows in the area where the sofas are. The father is sleeping on the sofa, the wife is lying in a chair, acrobatically contorted, and numerous children are lounging on a second sofa. The upholstered Söderhamn suite presents a different scenario: the father is lying on the sofa with a laptop, a child is asleep in front of it, a toddler is playing with an iPad, the blinds have been low-

Claude Parent,
living landscape,
1970
Claude Parent as a guru
at his home in Neuilly,
Paris, circa 1970

ered; a mother is nowhere to be seen. Here, too, the only windows to the outside are the computer screens, while the sofas, which expand to create upholstery landscapes, are above all places of immersion and sleep.

In the kitchen

Yet another piece of furniture that just keeps growing is the kitchen table. The Frankfurt kitchen, a hyperrational kitchenette for the modern home conceived by Margarete Schütte Lihotzky in 1926, had at best a board with stools. Ever since, the dining table has been growing and nowadays it is difficult to tell the difference between restaurants and large old buildings featuring living rooms that seamlessly transition into cooking areas. A super-size kitchen with a correspondingly endless, 16-foot-long fine wood dining table and twenty mid-century modern chairs from Vitra has become a status symbol of the urban neo-bourgeoisie, and a hotel stove with six to eight burners has become what the 8-cylinder sports car in the driveway used to be: a fetish, a way to reassure oneself of the good life.

There can be no objection to large dining tables, which may be seen as embodying a desire for experiences of togetherness transcending reciprocal visits of nuclear families. Even in the archaic single-room homes of the sixth century BC the family gathered around the *hestia*, the hearth in the center of the space.[26] People may perceive the relegation of the stove to a functional kitchenette as an aberration of Modernism and celebrate the cooking island, which even comes in room-size, as the return of an archaic and hence time-proven model of cohabitation. Too bad, though, that the owners will first have to earn the money to pay for all those fixtures and pieces of furniture: as a rule, this means that only one or two children straggling home from school will actually end up sitting at those opulent dining tables, looking at twelve to eighteen empty chairs. An almost biblical, dystopian scene: dinner for one, the twelve apostles expected to fill the other chairs are, unfortunately, unable to attend. A picture that repeats itself on six floors: a mere three or four people on altogether 120 seats at 100 feet of dining table, and no food cooking on forty rustic special-hotel-kitchen-gas-stoves. What these new dream kitchens illustrate above all is the misery of the increasingly lonely nuclear family. The commercial-size kitchen with giant dining table serves as the portent of a desire for community which, with the exception of a few moments a year, remains unfulfilled, because everybody has such a table and a huge kitchen. In the past there would have been only one of those in the street and it was called a restaurant. For the price of the commercial stove, the commercial refrigerator, the endless dining table, the chandelier, and twenty upscale, classic design chairs, you could have fed yourself there for half a lifetime.

In the children's room

The children's room is where what is experienced outside, in the adult world, is reenacted. Yet along with the toys that adults bring home for their children, life designs are introduced into a world that is still clueless about what life outside looks like, or should look like. What is played in the children's room both recreates and prefigures what happens outside: reflecting the present, it conditions the concept of what life could be like.

Anyone interested in knowing what will happen in the cities of the future only needs to look at the kind of cities that are built in children's rooms these days—and at the rules that apply there.

One of those cities is called Heartlake and was invented for the new "Friends" line produced by toymaker Lego. The "Friends" line of figures and pieces is one of the toy manufacturer's most successful products. They come as building sets that include houses, cars, cafés, as well as five girl figures. Lego provides the narrative that is to be reenacted in those building sets: booklets recount the life of the toy kit's main character, Olivia.

Olivia, age undefinable, part woman, part little girl, has moved to Heartlake City with her parents, because her father, a journalist, is starting to work for the "Heartlake Times."[27] Olivia "looks forward with great joy to all the fun and the pleasures the city promises." "Heartlake City," we are told, is a wonderful place with "many beautiful homes in different forms and shapes." The accompanying picture shows a hodgepodge of older houses and modern office buildings with mirrored glass façades. Olivia, we continue to read, wants to become a scientist, an inventor, or an engineer. In her spare time she builds robots. Emancipation seems to have made considerable inroads in the fictitious city of Heartlake. Both parents, the booklet explains, are hard workers, including Olivia's mother, who is a doctor. Their new home is located in a more upscale suburb of the city; it has a pink roof and "a large kitchen, a cozy living room, and Olivia's children's room,"[28] as well as a front yard and a vegetable garden. The picture of this dream-like suburban idyll shows the father handling a drumstick on the grill and the mother mowing the lawn.

Lego Friends

What ideal of a city, of housing, of living together does this introduce into the children's rooms?

Olivia spends her time exclusively with girls. Her girlfriends are Emma, Stephanie, Andrea, and Mia. Andrea, however, a figure that appears to be African-American, has to earn money "as a waitress at the City Park Café," where she makes cupcakes, washes dishes, and cleans the floor." Even in Heartlake City the prevailing relationship in the US between ethnic background and job qualification is perpetuated in a depressingly realistic manner: apparently, the only way for Andrea out of her social situation is a career as a show star.

The public life of the five girlfriends in Heartlake City consists in buying "cool accessories,"[29] while the fifth girlfriend, Stephanie, is a perfectionist and a "natural party planner," who bakes superb cupcakes, organizes garden parties, and (so as to avoid the image of a typical suburban housewife) also takes flying lessons. Stephanie is clearly closer to the suburban ideal of the neat housewife: she likes to wash her car "while listening to songs on her MP3 player," in the process finding that "car washing can be fun." In the meantime Andrea is scrubbing the floor at the café.

One of the odd things about the fictitious ideal city of Heartlake is that it presents unpleasant realities in the most cheerful tone.

While the white middle-class girls in Heartlake Heights live in large mansions, have horses and convertibles, and spend their evenings at garden parties, the African-American girl has to earn her money at a café. Strangely girly women or womanly girls, the girlfriends in Lego's "Friends" world sit all made-up at the café watching the African-American girl clean, or buy beauty products and clothes, all the while seemingly waiting for their men to return from work at some point. Rather than a playful utopia with a perpetual rebuilding option, as it used to be with Lego sets, Heartlake is a poured-in-place reflection of socioeconomic conditions in American suburbs.

"Go and build airplanes, animals, houses, cities!" a 1959 Lego brochure states encouragingly. In 2001, the Lego catalog for the "Bionicle" line explains what the goal of playing with the Bionicle figures is: "to break the hold the infected masks have over the Rahi." Only then will the magic light of Mata Nui once again shine brightly.

The world of a child is as boundless as his or her imagination, the founder of Lego, Ole Kirk Christiansen, once wrote: "Give free rein to the creative urges of the child and he or she will build a world that is richer and more imaginative than an adult can even conceive of." In view of the new gender segregation that Lego introduces into children's rooms, and in view of the extraterrestrial bio-monsters and rebel strongholds on the one hand and the pink-colored cafés where blacks clean and whites recover from combing down their horses on the other, one can only hope that Kirk's remarks are, indeed, true.

In the bedroom

Is a home without a bedroom conceivable? There are many things one can omit from a home: the hallways, the windows. But the option of retiring to a safe room to sleep?

For a long time and much to the surprise of many building historians, the inventories of homes in rural regions in Germany, such as the Low German houses, would feature tables, stools, and chests, but no beds. Where did these people sleep? The answer was surprising: in "wall beds that were set into the wall of the vestibule."[30] For this reason they were not considered furniture: the bed was an integral component of the house, an inseparable part of the architecture. People slept in the wall.

As of late the wall bed is making a comeback: the house that author and actress Miranda July had built for herself by the Japanese architect Yoshiharu Tsukamoto has no separate bedroom. It does have wall beds, though. In July's home the wall bed enhances the feeling of security and a sense of the cave-like. The house is atmospherically radicalized, so to speak: rather than providing roughly same-size spaces for working, sitting together, and sleeping, the living space is expanded to include an open terrace on the roof that is sheltered from the sun. This allows one to live outside whenever the weather permits, while the bedroom shrinks to the size of a snug corner hideaway.

Bed in July House, Nevada City, California (Yoshiharu Tsukamoto)

As a matter of fact, all historical residential buildings known today included sleeping places. However, the separate room for sleeping that is furnished with a single or double bed and which, as a rule, is accessible to no one but the users of those beds is a culturally rather new invention.

If one believes historical accounts, then what to us today would appear like an orgy was the normal state of affairs in the Middle Ages: it was allegedly quite common for "parents, uncles, aunts, cousins, children, slaves, and servants to huddle" in the same bed and, much to the dismay of the church, for "often more than ten individuals to sleep buck naked and higgledy-piggledy," Pascal Dibie writes in his "Ethnology of the Bedroom."[31] Yet, separable sleeping spaces have been around for a long time: on prints from the fifteenth century the lady of the house carries the key for one on her belt.[32] The bedroom was connected to the living room through a lockable door and it was the only place inaccessible to guests, whereas the living space was often more like part of the street.

However, not everyone who had such a bedroom defined it as a retreat: Francis I of France bestowed the greatest honor on his general by sharing a bed with him. Around 1600 Henri IV honored the philosopher Montaigne in the same way. René Descartes would lie in bed for sixteen hours a day and only sit up to write something down. The philosopher Thomas Hobbes conducted mathematical studies in bed and jotted down his ideas on the sheets. Louis XIV, too, turned the bedroom into a public space and positions such as those of the large bread cutter, the cravat keeper, and the night commode warden were sold to nobles for 100,000 francs.[33]

A broad consensus on issues of pudency, which could vary depending on social status, developed only in the nineteenth century. Erica Pappritz, the chief of protocol of the West German chancellor Konrad Adenauer, writes in *Etikette neu*, her book of etiquette, that double beds "are appealing," but unpractical: "two single beds, placed at a certain distance from one another, will be more suitable. They have the advantage of allowing the necessary physical separation in the event of illness."[34] The bedroom was thought of with the event of illness—rather than with pleasure—in mind. It was, if anything, like a penal sleep facility where you had to protect yourself against filth and illness. For this very reason linoleum flooring, which was flat-colored, washable, and aseptic, came to be recommended at the time.

Looking at 1950s advertisements for beds today, one wonders whether people at the time ever slept in beds. The covered beds stand still, clean and untouched, as if the sheets were enveloping a double sarcophagus. In movies such as the 1959 comedy *Pillow Talk* the bedrooms of the leading actors, Rock Hudson and Doris Day, are form psychograms of various stereotypes of masculinity and femininity. Doris Day, who plays an interior decorator, is lying in a pastel den of white-pink-cream-colored pillows and duvet gables, while he is living with jagged, gloomy expressionist paintings in an apartment furnished with earthy, green-brownish, whiskey-drinker tones and sleeping in a black bed with red pillows.

Later on, when she wants to take revenge on him, she decorates his apartment in "feminine" tones, a castration of sorts of the man's apartment that is thereby deprived of its smoky, dark virility.

The aesthetics of the bedroom changed only at the end of the 1950s when French bed manufacturers such as Treca pushed onto the international market. Suddenly, beds became colorful; suddenly, advertising showed modern women. And ever since, bed advertising is a reliable indicator of social micromovements, a mirror of living style ideologies.

As part of this trend the Ruf International Company turned the once stuffy sleeping area of the early 1950s into a space station: the bedroom as a total work of art looked like a giant yellow-white honeycomb. It featured a telephone made of glass, yellow-white wallpaper, spherical TV sets, and white leather chairs. At first glance all this seemed very exciting and modern. At the same time, however, the bright sleeping worlds that pretended it would never be night again were but the logical development of the trend introduced by Ms. Pappritz. The bedroom left the darkness of the private: the bed of the 1960s was the hood of the house. Not coincidentally, the same period saw seminude women appear both on the gaudy beds and on the long hoods of new sports cars. Mini fashion took disrobement to the street: sex left the bedroom and entered public space.

It was not until the 1980s that the liberal-libertine ideals were superseded by a neo-conservative economic pragmatism; and the ideological change was again nowhere as evident as in the German bedroom. The mainstream bed of the conservative revolution was the futon, which put people out of their crumpled pillows firmly back on the ground of fact again. The futon turned sleeping into a

Advertising for beds, 1970, 1973, and 1984

martial art. No squeaky springs. No baroque swinging of mattresses and hips. The hippie girls had disappeared from the advertising for these beds, as had the nice Che Guevara daddies with their naked little children. The futon was hard and so were the bodies on it: steeled at the fitness center, shaped by the determination to achieve.

The crisis of the private: the bed as workplace. The most recent advertisements and TV series are populated by people for whom the bed is no longer the place where you rest after work or where you have fun, but rather the workplace itself, from which people mail, sell, make phone calls, google. The bed resembles a soft desk and the most intimate spot has become a place of public communication. What does this mean for the notion of privacy? Things used to be clearly divided in terms of space: business dealings took place in the office, on the street, in public space. This was outside, in the public sphere. The house and especially the bedroom inside were places of refuge, intimacy, non-communication: the interior. The revolution in communication technology and changes in the law have bollixed this arrangement to the point that concepts are crumbling at the edges. What is the private sphere here? What does being private or public mean? What are people doing when, after sending mails and texts, skyping, and making calls for seven hours from their private rooms, they go out on the street without a smartphone? Are they leaving their private sphere and entering public space, or is it, rather, the other way around? The terms to describe inside and outside, private and public are eroding. What does this mean for the house, for the square, for the city?

It would be nonsense to claim that something is either private or public, just as it would be nonsense to claim there is only birth and death. What is interesting in both cases is the large space in between the two extremes. In nineteenth-century literature we already find that clear categories of space are increasingly being played with and shaken up. In her analysis of Paul Valéry's novella *Monsieur Teste* and Marcel Proust's *Combray*, Mary Gallagher has pointed out how, in descriptions of the theater and the bedroom, categories of the private and the public overlap. While Monsieur Teste is all by himself at the theater, as if in a shelter of privacy, the bedroom becomes the setting of a strange, almost Kafkaesque encounter with the narrator, in the course of which Monsieur Teste explains that he will now lie down to sleep, while telling the visitor he is welcome to stay, like in a public space.

Is an existence beyond the legal categorization of spaces as social, private, and intimate conceivable? What forms can, or should, architecture take for habitation at a time when the concept of privacy is changing radically as a result of the virtualization of the public and the interconnectedness in social networks and because of the increased possibility of being spied out through data analysis, technical surveillance, and data acquisition options—at a time when the concepts of private and public may, in fact, have lost their descriptive power as a binomial opposition anyway?

As early as the 1980s, the technological development of powerful directional microphones and thermal imagers made it possible for walls to be acoustically and optically perforated and thus to lose their physical if not emotional function as a shelter against being spied out. The "inviolability of the home" that is enshrined in Article 13 of the German constitution and that invariably presupposes an inviolability of the bedroom has been eroded. Following a 1997 resolution by the Bundestag, the lower house of the German Parliament, it is now permitted to basically spy out any suspect with directional microphones and cameras, even in his bed.

Thus the final envelopes of the private are shed, despite legal safeguarding provisions such as the German special right to informational self-determination, which was specifically constructed by the German Federal Constitutional Court. No matter how thick the pillows and walls: the state—or private agents such as Google, Facebook, or Nest—will always get through. Perhaps the new coziness, the aesthetics of isolation since propagated in advertisements for beds is a defensive reaction. As early as 1959, Ernst Bloch noted that the large picture window requires an "outside populated by attractive strangers rather than Nazis; the floor-to-ceiling glass door really requires sunshine to show up and enter, not the Gestapo."[35] Until the NSA wiretapping scandal this distrust had largely disappeared. The state was perceived as a guardian rather than an intruder and it was to protect the population from attacks, plots, epidemics. A majority had no objection to the collection of private data, if it served to make the country more secure. Contrasting with this need for security in actual space was complete self-exposure in virtual space. Securitate and Stasi agents would rub their eyes in disbelief in view of the scale of the most intimate information that citizens disseminate about themselves on social networks such as Facebook alone. This equanimity is gradually on the wane only because of the lessons from the NSA spying scandal and growing public awareness of the scope of commercial and governmental information and data acquisition schemes to help predict citizens' behavior. What the surrender of imperviousness against being spied out—the transformation of the intimate in the house—means for habitation has not yet been thoroughly researched. Yet the question is what could houses look like that respond to the changing social and technological developments?

Residential building, Tokyo (Ryue Nishizawa)

Chapter 3

Different Houses

Architecture and language

Designing has a lot to do with language: with the terms in which architecture is not just described, but also conceived. The work on form must be preceded by work on the concept (or by an intuitive ability to bypass the concept conditioning the design work while forming). Creative freedom requires the ability to overturn and reframe an established, unchallenged category. Yet the concepts that architects and planners operate with are oddly fuzzy. What does the devaluation of the wall and the reduction of the house to protection from physical dangers such as storms or home invasions mean? Whether people work at home, whether a bedroom is also used as office space, does have bearing on the question of how homes should be lived in and built. Down-to-earth definitions ("inside is where the rain doesn't reach") do not go very far in explaining things. All the technological developments fostering the dissolution of the clear boundaries between inside and outside, private and public space exacerbate the language crisis of architecture. What does protection or "inside" mean? When are we "outside"? What is "public" and where are we "public"? And in what ways can we be "chez nous," as the French call "being home": with ourselves? What other forms could a roof take? Is it possible to live in a wall? What would architecture look like that features none of the elements which usually make up a house (wall, door, window, room), while still being habitable?

An example of architectural thought that transcends the conventional terms of architecture is found in Japan.

Building beyond categories
Fujimoto's House NA

> *"We should learn to live more on staircases. But how?"*
> Georges Perec, *Species of Spaces*

A quiet side street in Tokyo is home to an unusual house that does not seem to have any walls or different floors. Hardly any furniture is to be seen and if some pieces do appear, they stand around like tourists who are lost. The house stands on the street like an idea that is about to materialize—and in the process eliminate the conventional notion of a house. At first glance, after the initial shock, the structure recalls a house that has lost its clothes: no walls wherever one looks.

House NA replaces the house as we know it—a sequence of 7- to 13-foot-high stacked boxes of the same width and length connected through staircases or elevators—with an artfully irregular sequence of plateaus that rise like steps. Where there used to be four floors, there are now twenty different levels that are linked in complex ways. The house resembles a climbing rock in which recesses open up where the children can play and adults can sit in the sun and drink tea; like a tree in which you can swing from branch to branch. Where there used to be walls, there is now glass. The house basically consists exclusively of window frames. Curtains provide for privacy and there are both snug recesses and open levels where one is as exposed as when sitting on a bluff overlooking the sea.

House NA, Tokyo (Sou Fujimoto)

Many of the designs of Sou Fujimoto, who was born in Hokkaido in 1971, appear so light, so clear, and so delicate that it almost seems as if gravity has slackened. The various parts of the house float in space, as if in a still of the slow-motion explosion at the end of *Zabriskie Point*. House NA looks equally unlikely with its thin-legged braces. Its elegance lies in no small part in the impossibility of it being there at all: its girders seem much too delicate. Even realized, House NA still looks like a computer animation, a built optical illusion. It takes the magic of the design—which invariably looks more elegant and lighter than its realization in the messiness of concrete, steel, and glass—and makes it a reality, while at the same time seemingly maintaining a utopian limbo between conception and actual form, design, and structure.

When talking about a "house," one thinks of walls, doors, furniture. Asked to design a three-story house, one thinks of stacking three boxes with a ceiling height of about 8.8 feet. Fujimoto takes a different approach, as House NA shows. He deconstructs the concept of the story or floor and shows what else can be created when dealing with a height of three "floors" and in what different ways this space can be configured—for instance, as twenty levels.

Fujimoto puts working on the concepts before working on forms. His is a kind of architectural thought that operates beyond the conceptual categories in which architecture is typically described and conceived, and it is in that kind of thought that the freedom of this new form of architecture lies.

There are numerous examples of such formal thinking transcending concepts of space in contemporary Japanese architecture and Fujimoto is one of their most important exponents. His "House before House" piles barely room-size residential cubes into an arti-

ficial rock, puts trees in between and gets the occupants to climb, as it were, through the branches of a tree. This house intensifies sensory perception: it brings nature into the city and turns the home quite literally into a living landscape.

Fujimoto's Final Wooden House, which he built in the woods of Kumamoto in 2008, is also a kind of thought edifice—a cube on a surface of just 86 square feet composed of 14-inch timbers that are artfully

House before House,
Utsunomiya (Sou Fujimoto)

stacked to create a spiral surrounded by intruding wooden elements. Inside this spiral you can lie, sit, sleep, or watch TV—in other words, do what is called "living"—on various levels. There is no furniture, though, and there are no walls or doors: the entire arsenal of objects and concepts used to create and describe a living environment becomes useless here. The projecting timbers replace furniture: they can serve as a table or, when covered with cushions, as a sofa and, when covered with mats, as a bed. The house questions the concepts used to describe and conceive of architecture. Someone planning a house automatically draws doors, walls, rooms, space for furniture. Fujimoto shows that this can be done differently. The house has none of the features that distinguish a house and yet it is habitable. It is like a sponge with life embedding itself in its pores. Fujimoto liberates architecture from the corset of concepts that impedes its possible richness, its reinvention.

Final Wooden House, near Kumamoto (Sou Fujimoto)

The same holds true for Fujimoto's House N in Oita, which, like a Russian matryoshka doll, consists of several artfully nested fenestrate building envelopes that are partly open, partly glazed.

House N is a stage rather than a hermetic object. It not only incorporates classic elements of traditional Japanese architecture, such as the idea of the *engawa*—a raised and covered intermediate zone surrounding the traditional Japanese house that can be added to the interior or the exterior thanks to sliding panels—and the effect of the classic Japanese room divider, the *shoji*, which allowed the house to be adapted to different needs and enabled the occupant to keep redefining the boundaries between interior and exterior.

The basic separation between inside and outside through a built wall with a door in it and the allocation of living, eating, and sleeping to different rooms does not apply to the traditional Japanese house. Often there are no designated bed- and living rooms. Beds are not visible, as they are kept in the *oshiire*, a kind of closet, during the day. Between the street and private spaces you find not just one or two doors, but rather a maze of thresholds: first a piece of semi-public space, such as a paved front area, then a gate through which you get to the *genkan*, or entryway, where you leave your shoes, and then, after a step leading up to the level of the living spaces, you enter the actual house. The *engawa* and the corridors can be closed with sliding doors and thereby added to the house or the terrace. Then there are the *shoji* and sliding panels called *fusuma* to subdivide the space.

House N, Oita (Sou Fujimoto)

In a theoretical text[36] Fujimoto lists ten themes of new interior design, including the nest, the forest, the cave, and the "guru-guru," the spiral. Basic gestures of building are illustrated: four walls are erected around a tree, making the tree the occupant of a space, a *hortus conclusus*, and turning nature into a garden, that is, private space. Fujimoto shows how architecture functions according to the principles of forest, nest, or cave: he designs models for houses that are made of compacted wooden sticks, houses that are piled up by stacking wood—for example, Final Wooden House—and houses that are created by digging a hole into a block.

Fujimoto takes the elements of architecture apart, as it were, and puts them together again in a looser and more open way—as a landscape, a stage, rather than a hermetic sculpture. His houses are flexible to the point of being formless. They are more like a frame waiting to be filled than a painting. They are reminiscent of the abilities of a sponge to absorb environment, to compact itself, to flexibly respond to changes from outside, and to be open. Their strength is in their weak form.

At a time when people's relationship to public space is characterized primarily by hysterical security efforts, Fujimoto makes his architecture relate to the outside in a different way. His structures are more open, maze-like, porous, and interwoven, and their threshold between inside and outside is rather like a maze extending in space that allows for a more playfully balanced relationship between the two.

Inclusiveness: the maze replaces the wall

Any boundary is more effective when the trespasser loses his bearings: the maze, the many-layered filter, is a better boundary than the wall which, once overcome, allows the intruder to access the innermost part. This dissolution of the boundary in a multilayered space can provide much more effective protection than that offered by pathetically thick walls and doors. In the traditional shop houses of North Africa the boxes with merchandise, which are placed closely together so that only little space is left for narrow passages to the warehouse, constitute a first filter. The warehouse itself is a deep maze that sometimes leads to a kitchen. There is not a single door between this private space and the street, and yet the inside is much better protected than by a door that is easily forced open.

House N teaches us the same lesson. The spatial depth of the filter zone is what allows for the feeling of nonclaustrophobic security. The relationship of public and private sphere can be controlled here, as there are different kinds of spaces—open, semi-open, or completely closed—for any weather situation or mood.

In traditional Japanese architecture the *engawa* was such a place: a flexible intermediate space that could be both, depending on whether the sliding panels were opened or closed. This spatial richness is also found in most of Fujimoto's buildings.

The occupant has an active role assigned to him: the space wants to be conquered, taken possession of. In his theoretical writings Fujimoto distinguishes between nest and cave as fundamental typologies of habitation. The nest did not exist before and is created to meet a very particular housing need. The cave, however, does exist before it is occupied. The occupant's accomplishment and, indeed, the architectural act consists in recognizing the cave as *habitable* and making oneself at home in it. This act of settling in is fundamentally different from the act of building and it can be argued that Fujimoto—who in this respect may be a contemporary Mannerist—has a great talent for building homes that, like a cave, like "found nature," need to be conquered anew on a daily basis, in more playful and unfettered ways than people usually live.

When discussing contemporary Japanese architecture, people inevitably claim that it "dissolves the boundaries between inside and outside," as if this were a quality that requires no further justification. It has become a strange fad among architects, students of architecture, and architecture critics to declare the dissolving of boundaries between inside and outside a key feature of architectural quality. Thus architects point out that the floor of their pavilion "is conceived as a slab extending into the garden that further dissolves the boundary between inside and outside."[37] A glass manufacturer points out that the glass surface slides "sideways and dissolves the boundaries between inside and outside: a perfect connection between interior and exterior."[38] About Tadao Ando's work we read that "the boundary between inside and outside [is] completely abolished."[39] And as the magazine *Arch+* sees it, the quality of Japanese minihouses is that there is no longer a "clear boundary between inside and outside,"[40] etc., etc.

But why is the "dissolution of inside and outside" per se a quality? Stone Age man would surely have been anything but thrilled about a dissolution of inside and outside by bears or enemy hordes.

So what exactly is dissolved here in what way, to what end, and with what result? A closer look at contemporary Japanese architecture at least reveals widely divergent typologies.

A theory of the threshold
On the aesthetics of the new Japanese house

Ryue Nishizawa's green residential tower.   The five-story house that Ryue Nishizawa built on a 13-foot-wide lot in Tokyo is a miniature high-rise of sorts. Each floor has a room. Connected through a steep spiral staircase, these rooms have sliding doors on the side facing the street that open to deep balconies which take up almost half the floor and are reminiscent of the small *tsuboniwas*, those 35-square-foot, oasis-like minigardens, which in densely populated regions of Japan serve to bring a slice of nature into the courtyard. Sometimes these balconies are so densely planted that a green curtain is created. The vegetation replaces the wall here. In addition, there are light curtains which can be pulled closed. The occupants of these outside seats are thus shielded from the city by something that existed prior to the architecture—shrubs, trees, rampant leaves—and by something that is subsequently installed in buildings: curtains. The house in which fabric and plants seem to provide the only protection is both shrubbery and tent and hence anti-architecture—a vertical garden. As if from a nest, you look through dense foliage toward the street. "The occupants can feel the wind and live in a space that is outside, yet wholly intimate," as Nishizawa explains his design—just as in Shigeru Ban's 1995 Curtain Wall House, in which a curtain replaces the façade, with only the most intimate spaces beyond it being protected by a folding wall made up of glass elements.

Living in the wall: Fujimoto's LA Small House.   When does a wall stop being a wall? What if it were equally deep, high, and wide, or if one could sit or lie in the window? Would this still be a deep wall or would it have become a room? What if the wall became just thick enough for a person to be able to lodge himself in its openings, as an object that separates spaces, to create spaces inside itself that are more than just wall beds?

An example of this paradox is provided by most old castles, in which walls are often several meters thick, a depth that allows window openings to indeed become rooms.

What would we get, though, if ten walls with openings were arranged into a maze? A super-wall? A house of walls?

What would it mean for residential living if people were to reside neither clearly inside nor clearly outside, but rather in an undecidable in-between? If a house were defined not as an empty space isolated from an exterior through four walls, but rather as an agglomeration of cells, as a sponge structure in which uses embed themselves? If you could live in the wall itself, if it did not separate an interior from the exterior, if this separation itself housed habitation?

Sou Fujimoto has designed such a wall house. In a hilly part of Los Angeles, on a lot that was considered to be unsuitable for a building because it was allegedly too narrow, he planned a multi-story wall slice consisting of fieldstones fixed with steel rods and a slightly triangular floor plan: a kind of monumental fieldstone wall in whose interstices living occurs. You climb like in a cave, or across the ledges and juts of a steep sea cliff, through the porous maze of the wall-become-space.

One could consider these buildings—houses resembling the branches of trees, houses resembling caves—successors of the artificial grottoes of the Baroque period and criticize them as escapist refuges or, indeed, as a romantic and essentialist reduction of habitation to archetypal spatial forms such as nest and cave. Yet one can also understand them as speculative models for a kind of habitation that, no longer dependent on the old ways of framing habitation, allows new freedoms and encourages new forms of existence. And what if one imagined this house as a model for an entire city? What if the house became a small city of rooms? What if a walled town like Monteriggioni, which is separated from the landscape, functioned like a large house, the houses in it like rooms, and the streets like hallways? What implications would this effect have for the sense of publicness and privacy?

For all their artful play with interiors and exteriors, the most interesting new Japanese buildings are essentially single-family homes. The main objectives behind their dissolution of inside and outside is to make small spaces seem bigger and more complex, to avoid claustrophobia, and in densely built-up areas to bring nature and a sense of openness and tranquility into the house. The promise of the new Japanese house recalls the dream sequence in Maurice Sendak's children's book *Where the Wild Things Are*, where the room dissolves and turns into an endless landscape in which a few puzzled pieces of furniture still stand around like lost animals as a last vestige of the domestic. What if this design for the private sphere were to be translated into the dimensions of a city, if one built a city out of such houses? What would happen if one were to dissect the categories used to describe and conceive of public squares and cities as Fujimoto has done with the concepts of domestic architecture?

What would happen if the idea of the open-plan house, which reorganizes privacy and publicness, were to be translated into a larger scale: the scale of an entire city district? What would take the place of the classic dwelling built around the ideal of the nuclear family?

Anyone who wants to know more about the possible future of habitation must take a closer look at the history of the single-family home—and that of its possible alternatives.

LA Small House (draft), Los Angeles (Sou Fujimoto)

A bear attacking people in the Stone Age
(from the French children's book *Au temps de la Préhistoire*, by Pierre Pelot)

Chapter 4

A Short History of the Single-Family Home

"The nineteenth century, like no other century, was addicted to dwelling."[41]

Walter Benjamin

How Neanderthal man
goes into the single-family home
The biologization of the history of habitation

A children's book about the prehistory of mankind includes an illustration that shows a dramatic moment:[42] giant eagles are circling above a waterfall; in the distance a glacier casts a cold light over the woods; the gray sky is bringing snow. Mammoths, a saber-toothed tiger, and a rhinoceros stand closely packed together; a herd of mouflon moves across the valley. A creek eats its way into rugged layers of rock. Nearby, a bear pounces on a half-naked man who, clad in animal skin, stands at the entrance to a cave and raises his right arm to belabor the beast of prey with a hammer. A blonde woman huddles in the cave entrance, holding a child tightly against her body and anxiously observing the scene.

The book's purpose is to explain to children how humans lived during the Middle and Upper Paleolithic Period, and it is this illustration in particular that sticks in one's mind, because it so obviously conforms to the stereotypes of more recent times: the man is out there in the middle of life, pursuing his heroic activities, as he defends and goes hunting, while the woman sits passively at home, sorting things back and forth and taking care of her child.

Based on what paleoanthropologists can tell us today, the illustration shows a world that never existed in this form at the time of *Homo sapiens* and Neanderthal man. Humans usually lived together in hordes rather than as nuclear families, and instead of living deep inside caves, which were far too moist, they would at most take temporary cover in them. Moreover, the diet of Stone Age man "probably consisted of berries, plants, bulbs, and eggs, as well as of rabbits, lizards, or birds, which were also trapped. Those who hunted had to gather along the way to feed themselves, and those who gathered at the same time hunted small animals in doing so," as Julia Voss writes.[43] In other words, there is no reason to believe that women exclusively gathered and left hunting to the men.

Men hunt, women do the housework
The origins of a role model

The illustration, in which the pose of the hero evokes less a prehistoric male forced to fight off a bear as one of the heroes in Jacques-
Louis David's painting *The Oath of the Horatii*, reveals something
else. When taking a close look at the illustrations that haunt school-
books to this day, one cannot avoid the impression that they, too,
were—and still are—part of an advertising campaign for the single-
family home as a model of habitation with a clear distribution of
roles. The obvious images created by the draftsmen particularly of
the nineteenth century to illustrate family life at the time of the
Stone Age indicate, if anything, that nineteenth-century habitation
models and then current role models were projected back onto the
Stone Age. In Marylène Patou-Mathis's book on prehistory the man
returns from hunting fish, while the woman carries berries in her
apron. On closer inspection these images are illogical: why would
the woman not hunt for fish as well while picking berries at the
creek, and why would the man leave the berries untouched on his
way home from hunting mammoth? Those looking out of the cave
in long-haired animal skin costumes are really the house residents of
the nineteenth century. Stone Age man lives the way people are supposed to live during their time: men work and fight and women stay
at home, in the single-family cave.

The single-family home is not an invention of the nineteenth century. Houses that are occupied by a single family—father, mother,
and one or more children—have always existed: even in ancient
Ostia, before the start of the major building programs at the beginning of the second century AD, people lived in a *domus*, a private
residence usually with up to two floors that was occupied by just
one family.[44]

These houses were, however, one model of habitation among
many and not the norm: the "whole house" that was occupied by
extended families dominated. In homesteads, farmers, farmhands,
maids, the elderly, and children lived together in confined spaces. In
castles and palaces, several dozen people would often live in a single
building. The campaign-like idealization—based on moral and bio-

logical arguments—of the single-family home and it occupants—the nuclear family—as the only appropriate form of habitation and living for man began only with the social differentiation accompanying the emergence of the middle class.[45]

Jürgen Habermas has described the contraction of the "whole house" in *The Structural Transformation of the Public Sphere*: "The 'public' character of the extended family's parlor, in which the lady of the house at the side of the master performed representative functions before the servants and neighbors, was replaced by the conjugal family's living room into which spouses with the children retreated from the household staff. Festivities for the whole house gave way to social evenings."[46]

From the mid-nineteenth century on, representations of prehistory supplied the biologization of this politically desirable nuclear-family life design, assigning the role of working breadwinner to man and the role of keeper of the home to woman. In suggestive images the belief that a society should be arranged into nuclear families living in single-family homes was elevated to an unquestionable and timelessly valid truth of human existence. The nuclear family in the cave is an instance of the kind of mythologizations that Roland Barthes described in his *Mythologies*, defining the creation of myths as a deliberate "loss of the historical quality of things." By moving "from history to nature," one "abolishes the complexity of human acts [and] gives them the simplicity of essences." A myth "deprives the object of which it speaks of all history," Barthes writes. In this way the single-family home and the associated distribution of gender roles, which was seen as desirable by conservative social reformers and industrialists of the nineteenth century, could appear as a contemporary implementation of a historical desire of mankind.

With reference to the theory of evolution and early paleoanthropology, the image of man as the one who hunts for mammoths or money and woman as the one who stays home and decorates the cave is declared an anthropological constant. In late eighteenth- and early nineteenth-century literature, contemporary models of society are similarly turned into constants of human history. A well-known example is Friedrich Schiller's "Song of the Bell," where we read that "man must go out / In hostile life living." In Schiller's work the separation of spheres of activity into public and private is accompanied by an explicit gender-based allocation: the lad "into life so wild doth roam," while "indoors ruleth / the housewife so modest." Architectural discourse was never free from such biologizations—not even today.

Biologically, the counterargument goes, the simple fact is that a man and a woman have a child and so, naturally, they are the nucleus of a society. Still, this is not an argument for the particular form the three-member group has to live in. On the contrary: why should said biological fact be an argument against a child growing up in a large garden with other children whose parents live with their friends in the adjacent dwelling units? Why should we not build such new villages, open structures, living landscapes, or homesteads in the cities? Similar biologistic arguments have, in fact, been invoked to rail against day-care centers. But whether a day-care center is a joyful place for joint adventures or a space full of bored, neon-lit little people depends on the educators and the working conditions they are given.

"Cottage Economy" and the consequences
An ideological history of nuclear-family habitation

The need to organize human beings into groups of isolated nuclear families, affording them special protection under the law as the alleged nucleus of society and placing them in apartments and single-family homes, which the man leaves for work, while at home a single individual—the woman—is responsible for childcare and household, is a relatively recent development. Prior to industrialization the norm was the extended family, the village community, and, prior to that, the horde, whose existence, if we are to believe paleoanthropologists, one would likewise be mistaken to imagine as a

William Cobbett, "Cottage Economy"

life in uniform row-house caves with barbecues in the front yards. It is perhaps no coincidence that the notion of life during the Stone Age, of hunting men and gathering and cave-tending women, emerged at the same time as the first major wave of single-family homes were built in the course of industrialization.

These homes were not particularly popular: workers preferred a life as part of an extended family, which was better prepared for the event of illness and loss of earnings, childcare and food supply issues. That the single-family home nonetheless prevailed was due not least to William Cobbett.

The son of a farmer and an innkeeper, Cobbett was born in Farnham, Surrey, in 1763. In 1792 he moved to the United States, where he wrote pamphlets against other Englishmen who came to support the French Revolution. This earned him the sympathies of the British representatives, who even offered him money to bring other points of contention to the attention of the people. Cobbett declined,

Popular scientific Stone Age scene from a children's book

but just for the fun of provoking he displayed a portrait of the British king, George III, in his window; this led to clashes with critics of the monarchy and he was eventually forced to pay a fine of 5,000 dollars. After returning to England, he started the conservative weekly newspaper *Political Register* and inveighed against the Treaty of Amiens, until he was thrown into prison for insulting the authorities. Yet Cobbett's pamphlet "Cottage Economy," published in 1822, is one of the most seminal works for the history of modern habitation. In it he explains, among other things, how to brew beer, hoping that home-brewed beer would prompt men to drink at home rather than talk politics at the ale-houses. Cobbett remained a contradictory figure until his death in 1835: he was, on the one hand, a protosocialist social reformer who called for unrestricted voting rights, freedom of thought, and adequate wages for all workers; yet on the other, he was a fierce conservative who considered anything which deviated from the preindustrial way of life to be evil and who could polemicize excessively against "false gentility" or against living rooms that were relabeled "parlors" and furnished with pianos. In Cobbett's view wage labor and its consequences were a threat especially for the patriarchal family model: women were not to act independently, nor be granted the right to vote, as the nature of their gender made exercising this right incompatible with the harmony and happiness of society.

The assignment of the role of keeper of the house to women is not an invention of the nineteenth century either. In ancient Athens, the public street space was considered to be reserved for men only; women were at best allowed to run errands and subsequently disappear into the courtyards. As Xenophon wrote in his book on household management (Oeconomicus 7, 30): "For a woman to bide tranquilly at home rather than roam abroad is no dishonor; but for a man to remain indoors, instead of devoting himself to outdoor pursuits, is a thing discreditable."[47] Still, women and men worked closely together in the premodern home, in the bakery, or at the farm. This proximity disappeared only with wage work, with work away from home. Now the man left and the woman stayed. The contemporary production of prehistoric imagery corroborated this new situation as a biological given.

Subsequently, the single-family home became what today, beyond the home, is the yoga course: an institution that is supposed to be a place of recovery from an accelerated working life and of inner preparation for the latter. "In order to survive in the world and be able to perform one's tasks, man needs a space of comfort, safety, and peace, to which he can retire, where he can relax and recover, after wearing himself out in the struggle with the outside world," Otto Friedrich Bollnow wrote as late as 1963.

This twentieth-century description reveals a radical change in the expectations of housing. Describing the home as a refuge from everyday working life only became possible once the separation of functions of workplace and sleeping place had been implemented—and once work was defined as an alienated activity that left a person with the need to recover and be comforted.

A peasant or a carpenter who had his workshop in a house where there was a fluid transition between living and working and where closing times did not apply would have had issues with this middle-class view of work and living. For them, working was part of living in the sense of the Old High German word *wuan*, which means "staying put" as well as "being happy." Longing for a return to this state may at first glance seem like a nostalgic dream of preindustrial life, yet the technologically advanced professions, more than anything else, make the separation of work and living appear like a mere episode in the history of habitation.

Collective living or individual home?
On the history of a debate

With industrialization, the problem of accommodating workers—not least in order to keep them from revolting—grew more serious. Cobbett's cottage theory was, among other things, geared toward strategies of preventing social unrest. The contention that a home of his own will keep the worker busy with small joys and worries runs like a thread through the arguments of his champions. In his study on the beginning of the systematic construction of single-family houses in nineteenth-century France, Roger-Henri Guerrand quotes the engineer Émile Cheysson: "A small home and a yard turns the worker into someone who can truly be called the head of a family, a moral and prudent leader with a sense of his roots and wielding authority over his wife and children. [...] Before long his house 'owns' him. It teaches him morality, settles him down, and transforms him."[48] Echoing these sentiments, Alfred Krupp in Germany quite explicitly called on his workers to stay home in 1877: "Talking politics in the pub is incidentally quite expensive; instead, you can have better things at home. When the day's work is done, stay within the family circle, with your wife, your parents, and your children. Find ways to relax there; think about housekeeping and education. This and your work should primarily be your politics. Thus you will enjoy happy times."[49]

A central figure in the nineteenth-century ideological debate about types of housing for the masses was the early socialist philosopher Charles Fourier. Born into the family of a wealthy cloth mer-

Fourier's phalanstery

chant in 1772, he lost his fortune during the French Revolution and made a name for himself with publications on "universal harmony" and "calculating social and erotic attractions." Fourier was considered an oddball: he filled the homes he lived in with indoor plants, thus turning them into accessible jungles, and every day he waited for the arrival of a patron who made it possible for him to work on his magnum opus, the *phalanstère*.[50] This so-called phalanstery was a kind of people's palace, a housing complex for 1,620 residents with a plan echoing that of the Palace of Versailles. The central wing was to house the communal dining hall and a library, as well as a conservatory (Fourier was obsessed with the idea of defying the seasons and being outside all the time, even while being inside. His homes were proof of this obsession). Manufacturing facilities and apartments were to be found in the side wings.

The influence of this notion of a collective housing complex is still felt in utopian communes of the twentieth century, for instance on Monte Verità, in various kibbutz buildings, and even in the Bauhaus in Dessau. There, too, the center of the complex is not, as is typical for schools of art and architecture, the drawing classroom, but rather the dining hall, the commons, and an auditorium. Like in a phalanstery, the fictionalization of life, the public dimension as a stage, and a communal dining hall constitute the core of the Bauhaus; other parts of the complex house the workshops and the cell-like living rooms of the studio house.

As conceived by Fourier, architecture for the collective was not limited to formal arrangements. Not just the means of production were to be removed from the private sphere in Fourier's wild architectural dream, but the bodies as well: a central component of this theory is free love. For Fourier, the rumors circulating about excesses and orgies at the court of Louis XVI were to become the foundation of a new community. The phalanstery was to become a Versailles for the people, debaucheries included.

Consequently, Fourier's main enemy was not the absolutism of the ancien régime, but rather the bourgeois society that emerged after its elimination. Everything the burgeoning bourgeoisie created in terms of forms, ownership structures, and values—private owner-ship, the suppression of sexual impulses—enraged him, but few things could incense him more than the "chaos of small homes, each dirtier and messier than the next," the "clusters of disgusting cot-tages"[51]—and the concomitant ways of life. In *The New Amorous World*, Fourier wrote: "Harmony will not develop if we commit the mistake of limiting women to the kitchen and the cooking pot. Nature has endowed both sexes equally with scientific and artistic capabilities."[52] Fourier, too, underpinned his social model with ref-erences to the early history of mankind; in *False Industry*, he demanded a kind of unconditional basic income for all citizens, arguing that self-subsistence is a fundamental human right, since the "prime natural right" to hunt and gather had been lost with civiliza-tion and needed to be assumed by its institutions.[53]

Communal living at the Bauhaus
Outdoor classroom at the Bauhaus (Alcar Rudelt)
Dining hall at Kibbutz Mechavia (Richard Kauffmann)

The leftist politician and utopian Victor Considerant (1808–1893) seized on Fourier's ideas while the latter was still alive.[54] Consider-ant energetically championed the construction of phalansteries that could accommodate up to 3,500 people, with running warm water in every apartment, affordable rents, and central heating. A communal restaurant was to offer inexpensive meals, made possible by bulk purchases.[55] As a representative, Considerant introduced a draft bill to the National Assembly in April 1849 that was to commit the French state to building an experimental commune for 500 occupants near Paris, but his motion was summarily dismissed, as was his support for women's suffrage.

A first project with a communal kitchen for fifteen families, from which Fourier quickly distanced himself, was realized in Condé-sur-Vesgre in 1832: after just four years, this phalanstery, known as the "Colonie Sociétaire," was dissolved again for the time being. Jean-Baptiste André Godin, an industrialist who ran a highly profitable factory for ovens and stoves in Guise, in the Département Aisne, and who joined the phalansterians as a philanthropist in the 1840s, was more successful. In 1853 he invested 100,000 francs, about a third of his assets at that time, to support Considerant, who had fled to the United States after the uprising against Napoleon III and wanted to establish a phalanstery named "La Reunion" near Dallas, Texas.[56] This project failed dramatically: the enlisted colonists knew hardly anything about agriculture, the soil was bad, and when a locust infestation destroyed most of the crops, the colony dissolved after just one year.[57] Godin continued to believe in the phalansteries. In 1858 he purchased 45 acres of land next to his factory and personally designed a phalanstery, calling it "Familistère." When construction was completed in 1865, the complex was celebrated as a sensation. The writer Eugène Sue memorialized Godin in his novel *Le juif errant*. In this book, the industrialist François Hardy builds a community house just outside of Paris for various living situations, with efficiency apartments for single people and two-bedroom apartments for families. The actual Familistère featured glass-covered courtyards and water on every floor, a laundry shop, a large pool with a movable floor so that it could also be used by children, and a garbage chute, the latter a novelty invented by Godin.[58] A collective cleaning service was to relieve the women of household duties and a day nursery was to make it possible for women to work. Residents could get drugs for free and, for two and a half francs a month, basic health care. There was a communal kitchen and a cooperative that purchased groceries for a reasonable price. In this way Godin tried to circumvent the system of intermediaries who made money by reselling fruit, meat, bread, and vegetables.

The French liberals felt uneasy about this brave new world: as Roger-Henri Guerrand shows in his study on the Familistère, protest was fierce. In 1866 Jules Moureau criticized that the workers "were given housing and clothing without having to haggle over the terms of their purchases. Communal childcare was a pernicious institution that deprived the worker's wife of the most cherished responsibilities of motherhood."[59] In 1905 Fernand Duval still lambasted such facilities for "hampering [the individual's] initiative."[60] Émile Zola was among those who visited the Familistère. In the notes for his novel *Travail* (published in 1901) he commented that there is "no solitude, no freedom" in the "glass house"; yes, there is "order, regulation, comfort," Guerrand quotes him, "but what about thirst for adventure, risk, a free and adventurous life?"[61]

Rarely did the desire—expressed from a secure economic situation—for self-determination, danger, and adventure as key elements of life clash so obviously with the vision of a life within the collective, the insistence on *privacy* and self-determination on the one hand with the idea of a solidary commune on the other. Between Godin and Zola runs the line that, to this day, separates the radical liberal from the communitarian way of life.

The alternative model to Godin's Familistère is the workers' village. In 1874 the chocolate manufacturer Émile-Justin Menier built a village for his 1,700 workers, which tried to reconcile both: there were community facilities, communal dining halls for the workers, schools, day-care centers, a free pharmacy, and sick pay for the workers. Yet in this case the workers lived in duplexes. A work of literature was devoted to this housing development, too: the novel *En Famille* by the French best-selling writer Hector Malot, which was published in 1893.

In Germany, skepticism toward outsize collective buildings and people's palaces took hold even earlier. In 1845 the editor of the *Zeitschrift für practische Baukunst* (Journal of Practical Architecture), Johann Andreas Romberg, wrote "that the lower classes live in housing that is too expensive and too inferior," yet he asserted that "the example of the barracks" was no good, because of the risk of too many conflicts between parties, "especially between the women using the washrooms," and because of the moral hazards, since it was no longer possible to properly supervise the children of both sexes. Moreover, infectious diseases would spread in such buildings.[62] Romberg instead envisioned medium-size buildings with five to six living units.

In literature, too, the single-family home now appeared as an ideal. In 1879 Jules Verne published one of his lesser-known novels, *Les Cinq cents millions de la Begum*. In this novel a French physician and a German industrialist have to share an inheritance. Each invests the inherited money in order to establish an ideal city in Oregon, at that time still a largely nonurbanized part of the extreme Wild West of the United States. The warmongering German, a man named Schultze from Jena, builds a vast and monstrous industrial complex that produces mainly military equipment. The workers of the arms factory live in "Stahlstadt" and fiery flashes streak through the ash rain of this Steel City. Their homes are "tiny, uniform, and gray, made of prefabricated elements supplied by a lumber company in Chicago.[63] Things are much more peaceful in Dr. Octave Sarrasin's "France-Ville"

Book cover of Jules Verne's
The Begum's Millions

with its "coquettish, dazzling white" houses.[64] Each family has its own house and each house has a front yard. The flat roofs with their asphalt surfaces are used as terraces. There are no carpets for reasons of hygiene. The largest room is the bedroom, and all residents do sports.[65]

Economic reasons for the triumph of the single-family home

In Germany, a first attempt to solve the housing problem through collective self-help was in the form of the cooperative building associations of the nineteenth century. Independent housing cooperatives concertedly purchased land in Hamburg around 1862 and in Karlsruhe around 1870 and then sold the houses that were built on it to their members. By 1873 there were fifty-two such cooperative building associations. With the amendment of the German Cooperatives Act in 1889, liability was limited to 100 marks and members could use loans at reasonable conditions from the state insurance institutions that were intended to promote "lastingly healthy and cheap housing."[66]

For investors, the alternative model of the single-family home was more attractive. As early as 1832, the manufacturer Jean Zuber submitted a position paper regarding a model home for workers to the Société Industrielle de Mulhouse. Collective housing complexes were rejected on principle: "Accommodating numerous families who do not know one another under one roof" could lead to "serious tensions." On November 30, 1853, with 300,000 francs as start-up capital, the Société Mulhousienne des Cités Ouvrières was established. Within ten years, 560 houses with a kitchen and living room on the first floor and three bedrooms and a toilet on the second had been built, with 488 of them having been sold at prices between 1,850 and 2,800 francs. By 1867 that number was already up to 600 and by 1895 ten percent of the town population lived in what by then were 1,240 of these houses, on which the investors earned a good return.[67] As a last vestige of phalansterist ideas, there was a public restaurant, though married workers were emphatically discouraged from visiting it and engaging in the "pointless distractions of a common table."[68] The idea of private existence dominated.

A fundamental problem of the single-family house already became apparent here: while investors in the Société Mulhousienne des Cités Ouvrières and the construction companies earned good money with the workers' houses, the wives and children of the workers often had to assist with work, because the husband's wages alone would not have sufficed to cover the monthly repayments.[69]

The new single-family homes of the common people, which Zola idealized in literary form in his novel *Travail*, were in reality paid for with great sacrifices: the carefree childhood promised by their gardens was destroyed by the oppressiveness of the excessive monthly costs, which also reflected the profit-seeking of the construction companies. The people who moved into these houses likely lost any desire for adventure, dangers, and the free and untethered life that Zola demanded.

Explosives against the collective
The Fountainhead and the defense of the single-family home

In 1949, King Vidor made Ayn Rand's novel *The Fountainhead* into a film with Gary Cooper as the intransigent architect Howard Roark. The film includes one of the longest defense summations in the history of cinema: together with his lover, the architecture critic Dominique Francon, Roark has blown up a housing project, because it was not built according to his original design. In his speech he makes a passionate plea against musty collectivism and for the independence and integrity of the individual. The greatest cultural achievements are seldom the work of collectives, he explains, but rather that of brilliant individual geniuses who have the right to defend their brilliance against the leveling effect of collective decisions.

It is part of an essentially similar Cold War rhetoric to contrast the endless post-1945 single-family residential developments in the industrial nations of the West as the symbol of a democratic constitution with the dystopian industrialized apartment block monstrosities which the socialist regimes left behind in the countries beyond the Iron Curtain. The fight of the phalansterians against the builders of single-family houses, of utopian collectivists against the representatives of a bourgeois society organized in nuclear families continued here in dystopian fashion: in the inhuman concrete shelves of the East versus the social isolation of suburban residents in the commuter-traffic-snarl-afflicted conurbation of Western countries.

Freedom or socialism was an equation that, at least from a Western point of view, also seemed to be reflected in the preferred residential architecture of the Great Powers. Accordingly, responses to collective housing are still quite critical today, especially since the memory of the hippiesque communes of the 1970s, where often more than a dozen occupants shared a single kitchen and toilet in an apartment in a dilapidated old building, is still too vivid. It is therefore all the more interesting that for some time now, especially in Japan, architects have surfaced who transcend these ideological rifts and who design a new form of utopian collective housing that, unlike before, also takes into consideration the right to privacy, withdrawal, and the personal.

Moriyama House, Tokyo (Ryue Nishizawa)

Chapter 5

After the House, beyond the Nuclear Family

What comes after the single-family home?
Extended families: new ideas for communal housing

A person attends a school, learns a trade, seeks a partner, has two children, builds a house for four, from which his or her dead body is eventually carried away again: this was the life plan that shaped the architecture of the suburban residential estates of the twentieth century. It was the actual plan underlying the semidetached house: the image of a society consisting of isolated three- to five-person nuclear-family cells. It was the plan around which suburbia was organized, until eventually it seemed that life with a partner and child in a 2,000-square-foot house plus a minivan was a fact of nature rather than a sociologically and historically quite recent form of habitation that, in view of ecological, economic, and demographic pressures, is in danger of speedily coming to an end.

Today, families have long ceased to constitute the majority of the population: census data indicates that the proportion of small households in Germany will increase from the current 74 percent to 81 percent in 2030. Particularly in the cities, single households already make up the majority. In Hamburg, the data puts their share at almost 55 percent and in Berlin even at 58 percent.[70] Yet this social development is hardly reflected in housing policies. As a result, the forms of housing offered to the residents of a city have less and less to do with the life that takes place in them: the retiree grows lonely in the large family home; the single mother cannot find a suitable place where her children can play in the courtyard with the other children; and there is only a slowly growing awareness that housing could be organized in ways other than glued-together nuclear-family cells. A possible form of habitation was at one point called the "extended family" and then—with ideologically rather than biologically kindred occupants—"communal living." Both came with disadvantages in the form of the repressive social control these collectives exercised. Is another form of collective living conceivable?

Manifestos for post-familial housing
Tsukamoto and Yamamoto

Particularly in Japan, treatises arguing against single-family existence have been written at an astonishing pace. As Yoshiharu Tsukamoto, the architect, theoretician, and head of the architectural firm Atelier Bow-Wow, notes, American-style single-family residential developments only started to be built in Japan around 1920 with the emergence of the modern nuclear family. "Each family bought their own electronic appliances, cars, and clothes and the number of consumers grew simply because of this need to buy all those things individually." Ever since, a large share of all salaries is spent on rent or real estate loans, cars, and furnishings. Moreover, the house increasingly came to be the domain of the single family and closed to the outside: guests were no longer hosted at home." Both economically and socially, this has, as Tsukamoto points out, disastrous consequences, which is why "the focus of housing has to be redirected to communal and collective aspects."[71] His treatise is intended to be nothing less than a manifesto for a new form of collectivity. But to what forms is this supposed to lead?

Tsukamoto envisions a radical reorganization of social as well as architectural and urbanist structures. Instead of dividing a city into streets, squares, and homes, new zones are to be created: small city-like houses where eight children from four homes can play in a protected courtyard; microvillages where the retiree, the other children, the unattached graphic artist constitute a surrogate family for the child whose father works in a different city from Monday to Friday, for the widower, for the visitor. Tsukamoto's city is built around a new culture of hospitality.

Another architect, Riken Yamamoto, wrote a similar manifesto. His "Community Area Model" turns against the focus of mass housing on accommodating families. As Yamamoto explains: "The standardization of housing units led, in turn, to the standardization of families that inhabited them [...] In Foucaultian words, housing became a training and disciplining device for standardizing families."[72] The nuclear family is declared the norm by the houses that are built, while deviating lifestyles are considered minority phenomena or abnormal concepts. In fact, Yamamoto notes, all demographic data contradicts the "one house – one family" concept and building policies are a governance failure. In Tokyo, the majority of households consist of no more than two, usually older, people for whom the isolation in single-family houses or apartments is a problem. With his "Community Area Model," Yamamoto instead proposes open structures where dwelling units for singles or couples can be incorporated into a kind of patchwork of workspaces, offices, daycare centers, restaurant-like community kitchens, and loggia-like semiopen spaces for multiple dwelling units, where people can barbecue together in the summer. These new clusters would allow people to check on their children or parents or meet friends on the park-like roofs during a break at work. The buildings adapt to varying housing needs: the separation of work and living has been dissolved as far as possible and a space can be turned into an office, an apartment for a friend, or even a workshop.

What this illustrates is a countermodel to the familiar attempts of solving the housing issue. Socialist as well as Western state building programs served mainly to create housing. Subsequently, supply units, such as a laundry shop, a shopping mall, schools, or bus stops for commuters, were placed around these shelf-like homes.[73] The accommodation issue was resolved and the city, as a jumble of work, housing, consumption, production, and constant condensations, superimpositions, and alienations of various activities, as a compression of different ways of life, was dead—separated into formalized functions.

Yamamoto's urbanism is the countermodel: each of his collective buildings potentially contains the entire complexity of the city; all spaces can be used differently; shops can become apartments or be both at the same time. A degree of uncontrollability and spontaneous proliferation is not just allowed but desired. As opposed to the "one house – one family system," which is criticized as being closed to the outside and isolated from it, his model is an open system that can be converted by the residents and into whose branches ever new uses can lodge themselves. Larger families can combine several cubes, with the spaces in between serving as meeting areas; studio apartments can be attached like modules when children or older people are added or when several people agree to a communal living arrangement. Workshops, kindergartens, stores, and offices can also be accommodated in the boxes, as can unconventional post-familial groups, such as the contingent of senior Japanese ladies formerly active in politics or artists who decided to grow old together. For them, the architect Moriko Kira built an innovative hybrid between a large single-family residence and an apartment building with ten apartments, each with its own small kitchen and small bathroom—and in addition to this a communal living room, an open-plan kitchen, and a common bath.

Sharing

The "sharing economy" and the new housing collectives

Homes are getting emptier. The record collection, the address book, maps, photo albums, the camera, and the game collection have all disappeared into the smart phone; the document files have been moved into the laptop, and magazines and books are now on the e-reader. The consequences of this electronic drain for housing have not even been properly analyzed yet. Things disappear from the house not just because they are being technologically compressed, but also because they are no longer bought but borrowed. Car sharing, bike-share programs, borrowing platforms offering power drills and other household appliances, the private accommodation agency Airbnb, where people who are willing to share their home with strangers can sign up—the advantages of the "sharing economy" are obvious: you only pay when you actually use the thing, which makes sense ecologically and economically. Cars usually stand around and incur costs; a car-sharing vehicle replaces five private cars.

Of course, this requires a pragmatic rather than an aesthetic way of relating to things. The question regarding the implications of the "sharing economy" becomes interesting when we assume that identity is constructed, among other things, through objects; that there is a difference between getting out a dusty, heavy photo album into which one had pasted pictures years ago and clicking through a

Facebook file with photos; between taking a car-sharing e-car with silly stickers on it to find one's way to a nearby bathing lake or taking one's own car in which the dashboard is still covered with the dust from the previous summer.

Yet what could be the implications of the new sharing culture for housing? Underlying this is the question of what form of ownership of things and space is important for the construction of identity, and what things and spaces in the world of sharing can be ceded to others, thereby leaving even more space for what is really important.

Collective housing: what went wrong?

The first examples of communal living—understood as any form of housing association in which individuals who are not part of one family live together—emerged as early as the nineteenth century when the "whole house" gradually dissolved and the home for the nuclear family became the prevailing form of habitation. In the twentieth century there are two basic forms of collective housing: apartment-sharing communities consisting of people who do not have enough money for an apartment of their own and utopian or experimental living arrangements joined by people who want to try out new forms of communal life beyond the dominant nuclear-family dwellings.

As a way of life, communal living does not have a good reputation: most communal living arrangements foundered on the horrible vision of sticky pots, hair in the bathtub, dirty toilets, and other shared items for whose maintenance no one felt responsible. Many see the unpopularity of the classic communal living arrangement as further proof that it was an ideologically motived aberration of the 1970s and that the single-family home or individual apartment is the proper form of housing for man.

Fierce criticism was likewise leveled at the first major reform-housing experiments and collective houses, which developed in various places between the two world wars—prior to the boom of communal living—such as the Kollektivhuset in Stockholm.

In order to understand why most modern ideals of collective housing failed, and at the same time what potential they still hold for a new public building policy, it is worth taking a closer look at those historic communes.

Kollektivhuset

In Stockholm, at number 6 John Ericssonsgatan on the island of Kungsholmen, stands an odd, reddish house with cell-like balconies. Designed by the Swedish functionalist Sven Markelius (1889–1972) and opened in 1935, it was occupied by an intellectual elite of psychoanalysts and educators, Nobel laureates such as the famous economist Gunnar Myrdal, and his wife, the peace activist Alva Myrdal. The Kollektivhuset realized ideas that have their roots in the utopian communal houses of the nineteenth century. Markelius, the architect, planned fifty small apartments that were reduced to the bare minimum: a bed, a desk, a cupboard, two chairs, a bath, and a toilet—more a luxurious hotel room than a classic apartment.[74] On the ground floor the building included a day-care center, repair facilities, a laundry room, and a communal kitchen with dumb waiters for carrying prepared meals up to the apartments.

It was a compelling idea: habitation was to be freed of all the nuisances that prevented women in particular from having a job: the promise was that, without the need to cook or do laundry, people could focus on life.

Many elements that also characterized the classic kibbutzim which were built since the 1920s—the central dining hall or "chadar ochel," central laundry facilities, the dissolution of the paternalistically organized nuclear family, homes especially for children—also informed the design of the Kollektivhuset in Stockholm. Yet in Sweden the experiment failed: authors such as Staffan Lamm[75] wrote with embitterment about a childhood under ideological reform pressure and many accounts about life at the Kollektivhuset read like shockers: the children of hedonistically cold-hearted

Kollektivhuset,
Stockholm
(Sven Markelius)

141

parents relegated to the day-care center, the occupants imprisoned in a madhouse of Marxist poets, intolerant sexual enlighteners, and tyrannically ideologized educators. The joys of raising children, of cooking together, of life in the large family kitchen: all this was over. Instead, a bare-knuckle functionalism governed all areas of life. Eating was nothing but intake of food, and living, nothing but waiting for the next work effort; furniture was barren equipment made of steel tubing in which people were bent into shape, like in clamps, for a fully rationalized life according to the dictate of increased efficiency. The steel-tube chair next to the sleeper, a seemingly liberating concentration on the basics to some, has a chilling effect on those who see in it the disciplining incursion of a heartless world of tubes, conduits, and machines into what used to be the snug preserve of blissfully lazy evenings on the nostalgic velvet sofa. The reception of the Kollektivhuset illustrates how one and the same architectural form can be interpreted—depending on one's point of view—either as emancipating mankind from the form of housing that made women in particular slaves of the household, or as the implementation of capitalist optimization processes in the private sphere. "Everyday life shall be organized according to the division of labor along the lines of industrial production," critics say, linking the Kollektivhuset to fascist ideology, which likewise demands "absolute commitment of the individual to the well-being of the collective."[76]

One does not need to agree on all points with the severe general criticism, but a look at contemporary photographs shows that the Kollektivhuset does have something hospital-like, something washable and fully disinfected about it. It is hard to imagine long evenings spent together in the community restaurant with its barren chairs; the communal kitchen is not a new version of the shared hearth in Whole House, but rather a food-preparation plant, and the furniture affects the anemic elegance of surgical instruments. For a place where an unanticipated, turbulent life could unfold, everything is too aseptic and too pietistically ascetic.

The flaws of this and other collective housing complexes are obvious: life is thoroughly rationalized; there are hardly any nooks that one can retreat to and that offer a degree of privacy and comfort; no really attractive place of open hospitality tempting one to enter the micropublic space of the house. The same applies on another level to the classic apartment-sharing community: if a person wants to be alone, he or she has to hope that nobody will mistakenly enter the room, or else slip away so as to remain unnoticed by the debating collective in the kitchen.

Could there be a collective house that avoids all these flaws?

The new housing collectives

The Share

The housing project "The Share" in Tokyo attempts to answer this question. For this project, a 1963 apartment building was redesigned so that the actual apartments became even smaller than before. Now they are reminiscent of monastic cells, albeit slightly more comfortable ones. Yet the open spaces thus gained on the various floors were radically remodeled, with the result that you feel you are in a luxury hotel or a club rather than in a cheap apartment complex, just as the overall project marks a transition from apartment building to hotel-like housing. The entrance is like a lobby with lots of glass walls and there is a doorman. What could be described as a "culture of entering," which in the functional buildings of the past century was gladly reduced to a dim minimal entrance for cost reasons, is thus revived. There are also shops on the ground floor and, on the sixth floor, a kind of communal living room—a mix between a club, a restaurant, and an artificial forest with hammocks—as well as a large kitchen, a space for theater performances and film screenings or lectures, and a library. At the top is a roof garden where the occupants meet or sunbathe.

When talking to the operators, the concept underlying The Share quickly becomes clear: they proceed on the assumption that especially in Tokyo, people spend far too much money on unused space and unused appliances and furniture. When they come home from work, they need a place of retreat. If they do not want to see anyone, they must be able to lie on their bed and snooze or watch TV or read in peace. That is what the small apartments are for. Yet those who feel like walking up and down a bit or enjoy briefly meeting with a neighbor can go up to the roof terrace or to the huge communal living room, eat there or simply lie in a hammock with a newspaper, thereby using spaces that in Tokyo only multimillionaires can afford. These spaces are reminiscent of landscaped interiors: here and there an individual sits underneath a tree; sometimes people meet, otherwise they go off to do their own thing. None of the depressing claustrophobia of some apartment-sharing communities is felt here—even though there are communal baths. For this reason The Share should be seen as a spatially more intelligent improvement on the dormitory, rather than as a model that can be identically recreated anywhere.

The Share, Tokyo

The Japanese project is interesting for two reasons. For one thing, it shows how the dismal functional buildings of Modernism can be converted and demolition avoided. For another, it demonstrates how the compulsive character of communal housing complexes is avoided through spatial organization. People can be alone in their cells and can leave unseen via the elevator: because the communal zone is situated above the residential and office floors, it does not function as a social control lock like the kitchen of an apartment-sharing community or the classic village square. Eating, lying around on sofas, and watching movies are activities that take place in the world of sharing. As a result, a space is created above the rooftops of Tokyo that strikes a balance: it offers community, yet without forcing anyone into it. The promise of anonymity, which was—and still is—a quality of the big city, is maintained. At the same time, The Share manages to create an atmosphere of relaxed togetherness in a space for the imaginary extended family of the complex's occupants, an atmosphere that is reminiscent of old village squares.

The fact that The Share is such a success that additional similar houses are planned shows how great the need apparently is for a reconfiguration of the intimate and the communal. The most interesting examples of architecture that attempt this are likewise found in Tokyo.

Moriyama House

One of the best-known cases in point is the house of Mr. Moriyama, even though the word "house" ineptly describes the building. When we met him in Ota-Ku in the south of Tokyo, he was just sitting in the sun underneath a kaki tree that grows between the ten merely hotel-suite-size white cubes that make up his "house," holding his German spitz on his lap. As Moriyama explains, the dog is named Shinozuka after a famous Japanese baseball player of the Yomiuri Giants. Moriyama used to work in his parents' sake shop, located on the same site as the house in which he was born. Later, when the sake shop had fallen on hard times and he was forced to seek a new source of revenue for himself, he had everything knocked down and this new house built. Moriyama recounts that he really just wanted a house for himself and one to rent out, but the architect, Ryue Nishizawa, convinced him to do something different: Nishizawa built him a miniature city consisting of ten one- to three-story residential cubes that rather look like detached rooms. Moriyama occupies the largest one himself and rents out the others. Nishizawa planned for two years, initially designing a house with outdoor corridors; subsequently, the corridors became small gardens and the

Moriyama House, Tokyo
(Ryue Nishizawa)

145

rooms moved apart and became small houses. Moriyama wanders among his cubes as if through a landscape; he climbs a ladder to the tearoom when it gets too dark in the living room in the afternoon; and when it becomes unbearably warm on the upper floor during Tokyo's oppressively hot summers, he goes down to the basement, where thousands of CDs are stacked underneath a Pierrot le Fou poster. The house does not need AC: it offers enough nooks for any weather conditions and moods. The corridors between the minihouses, which are open to the sky, are a kind of maze garden. Trees grow between the boxes. A tenant pays 800 dollars for a suite-size minihouse with garden terrace in the middle of Tokyo—for this amount you would otherwise barely get a darkroom in this location.

Moriyama House, Tokyo
(Ryue Nishizawa)

What is this? A new kind of living landscape, a stage set, a house whose corridors are unroofed? Or a small city with room-size houses?

For the first time we are in a living community, a commune that works—because it wasn't squeezed into the wrong architectural form. Packing together ten people in a formerly representative apartment originally conceived for a nuclear-family way of life with only one kitchen and one toilet inevitably gives rise to a claustrophobic basic mood, as divergent notions of hygiene collide. At Moriyama House this is different; here, a wide variety of people live together beyond any family unit in a very confined space, without going on each other's nerves like in a shared apartment, precisely because this patchwork of friends and disparate people is not squeezed into an apartment with just a single kitchen. Everyone has a microhouse with a bathroom and a cooking plate. If a person does not want to use the communal space, he or she can leave the agglomeration without walking through the social maze—which is also a revival of the lost Japanese culture of the *engawa*, the intermediate space between inside and outside that used to serve as a communication zone.

Of course, there are numerous models in architectural history even for Moriyama House: in the notion of collective life at the Bauhaus, for instance, or in the ideas of Japanese Metabolism, whose capsules were supposed to quasi-organically adapt to changing biographies and social structures. What is new here, though, is how a form of de-ideologized communitarianism becomes architecture—and presents a way of life that calls into question the imperative of the isolated traditional private home. With the my-home-is-my-castle dream being the architectural manifestation of a late-capitalist defensive individualism that has just destructed itself along with its occupants, a new alternative looms here for life after the collapse of an affluent Western society that, stubbornly and contrary to all economic and ecological reason, assumed a basic right to representative single-family homes.

On the roofs of the residential boxes, which can be reached via small ladders, people have breakfast in the morning sun, meet the other occupants, and have discussions with them, thus giving rise to a loose collective beyond a family association.

Communitarianism and the liberal concept of ideal housing

Up to this point people had to choose between the vision of an anxiety-free, welfare-state-controlled and, by tendency, disenfranchised life as part of a collective on the one hand and the liberal ideal of an adventurous and dangerous insistence on privacy and self-determination on the other: between Godin's "Familistère" and Zola's praise of the single-home adventure runs the line that, to this day, separates the radical liberal from the communitarian way of life. Moriyama House creates a hybrid that combines the advantages of both models and has immediately set standards in Japan aesthetically as well as in terms of a model of life.

147

Be it Takeshi Hosaka's programmatic "Inside-Out-House," the "House before House" that Sou Fujimoto piled up like a cliff of residential boxes, or Be-Fun Design + Eana's Soshigaya House, a cluster of four dwelling units grouped around a courtyard or "outdoor living room" that was completed in Steagaya ward in Tokyo in 2012: in dwellings such as these it is virtually no longer possible to decide what is "public" and what is "private." The private sphere is not shielded from the street by a massive wall, which is a social promise as well—a modern kibbutz, a shared apartment rid of the sense of claustrophobia, a new architectural solution for giving form to changed, post-familial ways of life.[77]

House I, Akita (Yoshichika Takagi)
House of 33 Years, Nara (Megumi Matsubara)

The village (de-)constructed

Many of these structures could be described as deconstructed villages: the forms of community building beyond family boundaries that one used to find in old villages and that today can still be found to some extent in southern Italy and Spain—cooking together, long dining tables, squares where people run into one another and sit down for a conversation—also exist in these new complexes. Yet, and this is the deconstructive act that reassembles the old structure in a new, more open and less repressive way, they succeed, unlike the new bohemian ruralization movement, in taking away the claustrophobia from this small-town notion of community and linking it with the urban promise of a liberating anonymity. In these designs

148

the village is both preserved and abolished: preserved in its communal structure and abolished in its often stuffy confinement.

The result is open communities that are able to respond more flexibly to changed living conditions: a mother of two who has to join the workforce again can leave her children in the protected community garden with her neighbors, instead of taking them by car to friends or to a day-care center. A retiree whose wife died can continue to live here, because the neighbors help taking care of him. In a classic single-family home the world falls apart for children when their parents break up or when their mothers or fathers have to work in a different city during the week: a sense of emptiness and loneliness sets in. In the collective housing complex with its interconnected gardens, in which ten or twelve children live, they are part of the extended family of the village. This post-familial quality of the new housing collectives may be one reason for their success.

Collective architecture in America
From Habitat 67 to the Star Apartments

The Moriyama principle has an early precedent in a far-sighted experimental structure that was built for Expo 67 in Montreal in 1967. The architect Moshe Safdie, who was born in Haifa in 1938, created a staggered cluster of dwelling units: the 354 boxes stacked in the manner of a staircase housed 158 dwelling units for up to 700 residents. Similar to Moriyama House, Habitat 67 leaves open whether we are dealing with stacked private residences or spread-out apartment buildings; whether these are still traditional terraces or a new kind of floating gardens and places for the neighborhood.

The design was too far ahead of its time; the economic and ecological pressure to compress that would have made it a success did not exist. Today, as people look for economical, space-saving, resource-conserving, socially flexible, and expandable forms of housing, this is an example they could draw on.

One person who tries to build on Habitat 67 and the basic ideas of Yamamoto's collective house theory is the American architect Michael Maltzan, who was born on Long Island in 1959. For the

Skid Row Housing Trust in Downtown LA, he built the Star Apartments, a complex of 102 dwelling units with a communal kitchen, a basketball court, a gym, a library, and community gardens. The structure consists of prefab components stacked on top of an existing single-story building and is supposed to accommodate people who are homeless or have just lost their houses. The building is one of the few examples of architecture that, beyond structures for the middle class, also takes into consideration those who cannot afford architecture.

Habitat 67, Montreal (Moshe Safdie)
Star Apartments, Los Angeles (Michael Maltzan)

Sharing space
Collective houses in Europe

The new forms of collective housing are not limited to Japan and America. In Europe, too, there are several examples, especially of joint building ventures—various people who join forces to build communal homes without a general contractor or real estate developer. The houses these groups build are cheaper and better, because the money is spent on quality materials or because they are able to save money, whereas real estate developers invest only the minimum needed on details, so as to not to cut into their profits. This is one of the reasons why minimalist modern luxury housing complexes differ astonishingly little from social housing and its cost-cutting dreariness in the details of, say, their staircases.

In Europe, too, there is a renaissance of communal building and housing with widely varying goals and ideas about life.

There are projects such as BIGyard ZE5 in the Prenzlauer Berg neighborhood of Berlin designed by Zanderroth Architects, for which 72 partners formed a joint building venture. This complex stands on a north-facing site surrounded by seventy-foot-high fire walls. Lying behind the façade of concrete components and large wood and window elements are three types of apartments distributed over two rows. Twenty-three 13-foot-wide, four-story row houses face the street. Each has a green roof terrace surrounded by walls. This garden, which in a suburban house of the same size would be squeezed between the toolshed and the neighbor's carport, is located high above street level and concealed from view. An almost 14-foot-high living-kitchen area opens to a community garden located between the two rows of houses, and even if the execution looks rather reductionist, the basic idea is clever: the kitchen transitions to a protected communal space that is isolated from the city and in which children can run around and embark on exploration adventures unsupervised. In addition, the 2,700-square-foot roof terrace includes a community summer kitchen for joint parties and barbecue dinners. A form of casual neighborship results, a street lined by open kitchens; the children can play in large numbers and without worries in the 14,000-square-foot unparceled urban paradise garden. Located by the rear fire wall across from this are three low-cost three-story summerhouses and, on top of them, three-story penthouses that share a common roof terrace. In its design, BIGyard ZE5 combines the advantages of suburban row houses with an urban park-side housing complex and a high-rise with roof terrace—with the prices for the units being well below market level.

While the occupants of the Prenzlauer Berg complex constitute a rather loose, pragmatic collective that left the design details to the architects, the members of the joint building venture behind the R50 project in Berlin's Kreuzberg neighborhood were more closely involved in the design process.

Together with nineteen parties of a building cooperative, the architects ifau and Jesko Fezer + Heide & von Beckerath designed a six-story building that centers on the concept of communal spaces.

151

The entrance is below street level and leads to a two-story common room that serves as a large collective children's room or can be used for parties or meetings of the community. The apartments are located in a classic reinforced concrete shelf. The materials are deliberately plain, with concrete and a modular wood façade reminiscent of American single-family housing dominating. Here, too, there is a communal summer kitchen on the roof terrace and a common workshop in the basement.

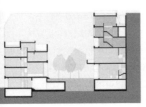

Zelter Strasse joint building venture, Berlin (Zanderroth Architekten)
R 50 joint building venture, Berlin (ifau and Jesko Fezer + Heide & von Beckerath)

Instead of individual balconies, each floor has a wrap-around, collective balcony the width of an arcade that allows occupants to pass by all spaces. Each window thus becomes a door to the in-house street; apparently, the idea here is to facilitate new lifestyles and new demands. In 1972, Ricardo Bofill already attempted something similar with his housing project Walden 7 near Barcelona, a 446-unit high-rise complex of eighteen towers named after B.F. Skinner's science-fiction novel, *Walden Two*, about a utopian commune. Here, too, the towers are connected with wrap-around common balconies, patios, and footbridges on which the everyday life of the community was to take place.

Yet even with the most progressive joint building ventures there is a basic psychological obstacle that stands in the way of more radical designs: the square footage fetishism of the parties involved. Instead of distributing the entire available square footage among all eight parties so that each apartment would have about 1,075 square feet, the size of the apartments could be limited to 650 to 800 square feet; the 400 to 275 square feet per party that would be freed up this way would be used for multilevel gardens, terraces, and a semipublic bar with a café on the ground floor. Such designs usually come to naught, as the parties ultimately insist on apartments that are as large as possible and have suspended balconies that look like half-open drawers of a dresser, from which the occupants warily peek into the collective space. What is ignored is that a smaller apartment with narrower and even cozier sleeping rooms—that is, an enhanced protection zone of the private and intimate—and a large floating garden, a more decisive form of micropublic space, would ultimately sell better than the same old residential drawer; the square footage fetish is more powerful than the architectural imagination.

A much-discussed example of new forms of housing in Europe is the building of the Kalkbreite cooperative in Zurich. Established in 2007 as a combination of potential tenants, neighborhood residents, and the Dreieck and Karthago cooperatives, about fifty people participating in a public workshop jointly drew up a proposal to build a housing complex on the site of a former streetcar yard. A year later the state-owned site was handed over to a nonprofit organization and the 850-member Kalkbreite cooperative applied to the City of Zurich to obtain the development right for a mixed-use housing and commercial complex on Kalkbreite, which opened in 2014.

The three levels in the area of the old tramway hall are reserved for work and trade; offices and workshops ranging from 270 to 9,700 sqare feet can be leased here. The main entrance to the building—an area that includes a front desk, a cafeteria, and a laundromat—is located on the third floor and is reached via a large terrace that is supposed to serve as a public square, but because it is located at such a high level it actually ends up reinforcing the building's fortress-like quality: aside from cafés, bars, and shops in the basement, the Kalkbreite is rather a citadel, albeit one that is all the more open to the inside: a day-care center, a communal kitchen, and the dining hall of the so-called large household are all located adjacent to the terrace; the small apartments which are, like all other apartments, located on the top four floors have been combined into dwelling clusters with common living rooms—again the principle of the residential community, here expanded to include personal bathrooms and toilets. A similar spatial organization is found in the riverfront buildings for Berlin-based joint building ventures that were realized

Kalkbreite cooperative, Zurich
(Müller Sigrist architects)

by Fatkoehl Architekten in cooperation with BAR architects and Silvia Carpaneto architects: here, too, there are classic small apartments, as well as numerous communal areas and "option spaces" on the ground floor which, rather than being used for shops, can be made accessible to the public, for parties, exhibitions, large community meals for instance—like an expansion of the city into the building. A person who owns a 540-square-foot apartment can use 1,600 square feet of common space, the roof terrace, washing facilities, a restaurant-size living room. Here, the key to affordable housing is the externalization of many functions that do not necessarily have to happen in the private realm, and a state-funded program for energy-saving construction as an ideal source of financing for the cooperatives' construction loan. For a 540-square-foot unit, construction costs were 185 euros per square foot, and a share of 100,000 euros is obtained for the cooperative. "This means that the cooperative receives an efficiency loan of more than 50,000 euros. With 10,000 euros of equity capital, one can take out a loan to acquire cooperative shares of up to 50,000 euros. Out of the entire stake, 90 percent is financed with an average interest rate of 2.3 percent for Spreefeld, as Angelika Drescher and Christian Schöningh explain.[78] Central to all cooperative joint building projects of this kind is the elimination of profit. The German joint building venture or building cooperative has nothing in common with building associations whose members rent or sell the apartments when they are completed. The cooperative as a legal form wants to make living space affordable to its members who are both co-owners and owner-users, paying a use fee to the cooperative; people are legally prevented from speculating with their residential property. The ideal is a stable group of occupants who live together over a longer period of time. The disadvantages of this model are obvious in view of the high fluctuation of city dwellers; under some circumstances the joint building venture can be an almost reactionary rural model that does not allow anyone to peel off.

Spreefeld, Berlin
(architecture: carpaneto architekten,
fatkoehl architekten, BARarchitekten,
program/project/process:
die zusammenarbeiter)

Another way to provide affordable housing is the housing model *Grundbau und Siedler* (basic structure and settlers) which the architects Anne-Julchen Bernhardt and Jörg Leeser put up for the International Architecture Exhibition in Hamburg: in this case the architects provide a concrete shelf in the mold of Le Corbusier's Maison Dom-Ino, as well as infrastructure, and the occupants build their own dwellings into it, not unlike Peter Stürzebecher's once revolutionary do-it-yourself building cooperative, which tried out participative self-management in the housing shelf at 116 Admiralstrasse in Berlin and inserted the desired dwelling cells as timber structures into the steel and concrete shelf.

One of the most interesting joint building venture projects is currently being realized on Kurfürstenstrasse in Berlin. The 36,600-square-foot building designed by June 14 Meyer-Grohbrügge & Chermayeff provides space for twenty-three housing units. These units interlock across multiple levels in such artful ways that the occupants have the option to either completely isolate themselves—in which case the house would be a normal apartment building—or to merge spaces such as kitchens and living rooms. This makes it possible for, say, a group of seven friends, three single parents with five children, or six octogenarians to cohabitate. The structure is modular and allows for a wide range of uses and varying options of isolation and openness.

"The house consists of six towers, placed according to the curve of the surrounding roads, forming a semicircle around an inner courtyard. The six towers overlap both vertically and horizontally, there are no clear boundaries between the different units/apartments, and the structure of the house can be seen as one large, single space continuum," the architects explain. "This simple principle leads to endless variations of organization and spatial combinations. Within the overlaps, each individual apartment has its own personal spatial conditions and they all consist of one very high and one lower space. Some units are also connected to each other by a shared space and they all have a close relation to the inner courtyard garden, shared rooftop terraces, and other public spaces within the building. Neither the cohabitation nor the sharing is enforced by the architecture, although the flexibility allows the inhabitants within the building to create their private and shared spaces according to their own particular needs."

In the cases where it does succeed, such new collective architecture provides the design for housing complexes that could also accommodate larger groups of friends and interfamily residential clusters, singles and families, retirees and transients. It overcomes the fortress-like isolation of the private without abandoning a core zone of the intimate. It costs less. It creates more freedom. What is tried out above all in structures such as Moriyama House is relaxed collective living: the six tenants have breakfast together, there are barbecue dinners and film screenings where the films are projected on the walls of the cubes. The modest Mr. Moriyama of all people is now worshiped as a prophet of the new collectivity that takes on wondrous forms in Japan: the loggias of the rigid high-rises that Riken Yamamoto built for the Shinonome/Canal Court neighborhood in Tokyo are, on closer inspection, what the village square used to be. And Junya Ishigami's new retirement home will not be a soulless concrete slab, but rather a village the architect assembles from recycled tear-downs throughout Japan.

The new Japanese house, in particular, demonstrates that one should not put all the money in the dwelling and its accompanying apparatuses (furniture, kitchens, second car). It caters to a different concept of living together beyond the biological boundaries of the nuclear family and reduces the pressure on the latter, which in the private home also constitutes the whole world. We know this from

Christmas celebrations: while even the slightest discord promptly lends a grim and claustrophobic note to the otherwise tranquil get-together of father, mother, child, and grandma, large family celebrations with friends offer more opportunities to briefly step away and retreat from the group, to take in the whirring, the noise and the glitter. The get-together of a large family with many friends creates the kind of atmosphere that is found in a city—which provides space for anonymity as well; people do not sit silently on top of one another; there is noise; there are surprise guests, children frolicking around, spurred on by the buoyant chaos. Ideally, a notion of hospitality arises that breaks open the closed space of the family.

This kind of social ideal is adumbrated in Japanese collective buildings, where the reorganization of inside and outside shows that a virtual large family of ten or twenty people does not have to end in a psycho-kolkhoz. They are not directed against the concept of the nuclear family—it is just that they also offer space to those living differently.

It would be wrong, however, to see something unprecedented in these designs: although formally different, all these avant-garde architectures rediscover an old quality of the city that was lost only in the course of industrialization with the reduction of residential architecture to boxes for the small nuclear family.

Woman on a bed with her laptop

Chapter 6

Transformations of Privacy

Openness and intimacy

For a long time there seemed to be no question about what is "private" and what is "public." The single-family home or the apartment is more of a private space, while the square in front of the city hall is public space. The private is what does not concern anyone else; public is what concerns many or all. When we go shopping, sit in a café, meet colleagues or friends on the street in a sphere of communication, we are in public space. When we lie in bed at home, we are in our private space.

When talking about the private and the public, we tend to think in spatial categories. The square, the street, the workplace (with certain qualifications), the restaurant—those are public. The apartment or residence and the bedroom, on the other hand, are private. Yet even at this point things are complicated.

In defining privacy, lawyers by no means limit the private sphere and the constitutionally guaranteed "inviolability of the home" to the physical home. A confidential conversation on an empty square on an early Sunday morning may enjoy the same legal protection as an exchange of words in the bedroom. A couple who invites friends over to their home will tell their child not to pick his or her nose "in the presence of others," thus defining the gathering of friends for the child as a public situation of sorts, yet at the same time they will tell a colleague that they want to remain among themselves.

This would tie privacy primarily to spaces rather than to situations and a need to retreat. Yet what are the implications of technological change for the spaces we live in and previously considered "private"? Is a person more "private" when walking along a street without a smartphone, or sitting in a crowded restaurant and paying in cash, or when that person is at home surfing the Internet and buying things online?

The private and the public are not basic anthropological constants either, but rather historically established concepts subject to social and technological change.

One of the fundamental problems of contemporary architecture and urban planning is the uncertainty about what can even be defined as private today or as public; what forms of being together and being alone exist and what forms can or should buildings and cities consequently take. Architectural theory refers with astonishing consistency to the seminal studies of the 1960s in this respect: to Habermas's *The Structural Transformation of the Public Sphere*, Sennett's "tyranny of intimacy," and Jane Jacob's *The Death and Life of Great American Cities*.

The meaning of what is "private" shifts with social and technological changes, as well as with the rituals that shape habitation. The new technological communication media and social networks are changing the notion of private space in much the same way that the emergence of television shifted family life from the eat-in kitchen, where people would sit across from one another for quite some time in the evening, toward the cocktail table, where family members now no longer sit across from but rather next to one another and look in the same direction—just like the occupants of the automobiles for the masses that emerged at the same time and brought them to the suburban homes with their TV couches.

The history of privacy and publicness is also a history of conflicting notions of what people should and should not do in a society. This is illustrated by a famous, rather extreme instance from the time of Henry IV of France when, during a meeting between the Venetian ambassador and the French queen, the latter "let a bout of acute diarrhea run its course," causing the ambassador to throw up.

Dwelling areas and workshops were often connected and open to customers even late at night: "In early industrial decades there were no specific regulations regarding working hours in the crafts. People worked as long as the master deemed necessary based on the order situation. [...] Working and living were closely related. As noted earlier, 'dwelling' often took place in the workshop. And the workshop was open to the outside world—especially, of course, to customers. Yet customers were often neighbors and acquaintances" and, as a result, "the openness toward the street that was characteristic of artisanal 'working/dwelling' occurred not just during the long workday, but also afterwards."[79]

The classic house was by no means a "private" place per se. A strict division between working and dwelling, private and public did not exist yet. Even the upper-class home was not private in the strict sense: servants, governesses, private tutors, cooks were present in the spaces, parlors, and studies. And the "drawing rooms" (from "withdrawing") to which the ladies retreated after dinner were quasi-public places. Craftsmen, workers, and peasants shared their homes with bed lodgers, journeymen, apprentices, farmhands, and maids. For millennia this combination of working and dwelling was a feature of most homes. A privilege reserved to castles and aristocratic residences only was the bower or ladies' chamber, a place of retreat heated with a fireplace and clearly defined as a private place that offered both warmth and isolation from all others.

It was only in the early modern age that an aversion toward the openness and indeterminateness of the traditional home developed. In Adalbert Stifter's novel *Indian Summer* (*Der Nachsommer*) we read: "He couldn't stand 'mixed rooms,' as he called them—rooms that were used for several things such as a combination bedroom-playroom or the like. He would often say: 'Everything and every man can be only one thing, but he must be that with all his heart and soul.'"[80]

Early history of private housing

The emergence of the Greek city was closely linked to the situation of the working population and the rise of the crafts. At the beginning of the fifth century BC "only a small group of aristocratic citizens still received income from manors in the Attic hinterland."[81] Life in the city was characterized mainly by craftsmen and tradesmen, as well as by artists who "had come into money and achieved social standing."[82]

Master craftsmen settled near the *agora*, in what was really a residential neighborhood. They opened their workshops and stores in the spaces between the dwelling and the street. These business premises were flexible and could be added either to the dwelling or to the work area as needed.

It would be wrong to assume that ancient houses that were occupied by a "family" were single-family homes in the modern understanding of the term. In the ancient city of Amarna on the Nile, the small houses formed "clusters that suggest extended families."[83] The public fountains served as meeting points for the population.

Amarna had about 20,000 residents, who lived in, among other dwellings, single-story homes with 385 to 645 square feet of living space.

Among the early Greek settlements of the eighth century BC, two fundamentally different typologies can be distinguished:[84] on the one hand, settlements with individual, detached houses, like in Emporio on the island of Chios, where the houses lay far apart, or in Dystos in Euboea, where small houses were found on the slope of a mountain; and on the other hand, compact settlements or agglomerations with houses crammed together, which developed, for instance, on the islands of Donousa, Andros, and Crete. Among the archaic settlements on the Halikarnassos peninsula, homesteads were found that consisted of four to six spaces grouped around a courtyard.[85]

"Private" and "public" were also defined very differently in the large houses of the Archaic period: one encounters a large number of rooms grouped around a courtyard that relate to the latter like a house to a square and it seems that the social mix in the house mirrored the city as a whole. "Maids and menials lived, probably closely packed together, right next to the *oikos*, the main living space."[86] Public life took place in this large room: guests were welcomed, poets recited their songs. Going by the findings of ancient studies, there was no gender-based segregation yet in the houses of the Archaic period. The *andron*, a part of the house reserved for men, did not exist yet and women "moved among men without any inhibitions."[87] It was only by the mid-seventh century BC that owners of small houses also had *andrones* added. "If this was not possible for lack of space, homeowners did not shy away from incorporating a banquet room into the *oikos*. This was done at the expense of the family room of which practically just a small angular remainder would be left."[88] It was only at this point that the spaces in the house were classified as more public rooms reserved exclusively for men and more private rooms. The *andrones* were where the symposia took place, at which the men dined and drank, sang and debated.[89]

Hence, the "private" and the "public" within the house were, in this case, not something that had always existed and that could be traced back to some anthropological constants such as a "need for protection." They were the result of a clearly identifiable historical process of development driven by clearly identifiable interests of a particular group of people.

So what does the designation of something as "private" or "public" mean at all today, and who has an interest in rendering a real or alleged dichotomy of privacy and publicness visible or, alternatively, invisible—and with what values and views of life in mind?

It is astonishing that these two concepts, which play such a central role in the debate about big-data attacks and social networks, are not defined with much greater precision, especially since there is an increasing understanding in sociology and philosophy that the concepts themselves are problematic. The philosopher Raymond Geuss, for instance, states: "There is no such thing as *the* public/private distinction, or, at any rate, it is a deep mistake to think that there is a single, substantive distinction here that can be made to do any real philosophical or political work. [...] Rather, *first* we must ask what this purported distinction is *for*, that is, *why* we want to make it at all"—what purposes and moral values it involves.[90] When a person is asked why one is not supposed to interfere in this or that and he or she answers, "Because it is private," this person is ultimately just saying, in a tautological manner, that you should not interfere because you think you should not interfere in such matters. The question why this is so remains open; what exactly does the right to privacy mean, for instance? The distinction between private and public has no anthropological status.

If we go along with Geuss, we can pinpoint an exact date for the first reference to a "right to privacy": the year 1890. At the time, the wife of Boston attorney Samuel D. Warren, a rich society lady, gave lavish parties which local newspapers reported on in great detail, much to Mrs. Warren's chagrin. Together with his law partner, Louis Brandeis, "her husband set about concocting a reason for imposing restrictions on such reporting."[91] The two published an article in the *Harvard Law Review* titled "The Right to Privacy," which in the United States still informs the concept of privacy today.

According to Geuss's account, the "right to privacy" was first claimed in the context of a media scandal that seems strikingly contemporary: as a right of defense of well-to-do people against the curiosity of a host of less affluent readers. This implies that the call for a private sphere occurred in a situation of visible social inequality and that it was closely linked to property and the need to shield it. One could argue that Émile Littré already raised a similar claim in his *Dictionnaire* (1863–72), where we read: "Private life needs walls around it. No one is allowed to spy out or divulge what happens in the home of a private citizen." Interestingly and no matter whether you take its definition of 1820 or that of 1890, the "right to private life" as it developed in civil society and liberalism conflates psychological with spatial categories: the interior, being alone, as a prerequisite for identity. Accordingly, the upper class introduced capsules of privacy into the new spheres of the nineteenth-century public world, which were meant to maintain a being-among-ourselves: first-class ship cabins and train compartments, private baths and conservatories, and the private box in the theater.

Utopian dreams of utter publicness

In the classic utopias, on the other hand, there is no privacy. In the great utopian novels of the sixteenth to nineteenth centuries, such as More's *Utopia* of 1516, Vairasse d'Alais's *History of the Sevarambians* of 1702, and Rétif de la Bretonne's *Southern Discovery* of 1781, people live in collectives that do not show signs of any form of privacy.

"Every house has a door to the street and another to the garden," we read in Sir Thomas More's *Utopia*. "The doors which are made with two leaves, open easily and swing shut automatically, letting anyone enter who wants to—and so there is no private. Every ten years, they change houses by lot."[92] A garden for sports, play, and cultural presentations is intended to prevent any privacy; there are courtyards and community rooms.

The degree of perfection of a society is imagined as a state where there is no longer a need for any privacy. People eat together and celebrate together; the houses in *Utopia* have no shutters and small doors—nobody can hide. In the "Addendum to the Journey of Bougainville" even the act of sexual intercourse is performed in public space, spurred on by the collective: "The transparency of hearts is revealed in public space, defined and controlled by the state,"[93] Jean Marie Goulemot notes, pointing to the similarity between the utopian worlds and the model of the absolutist state. "Privacy is not defined, as in Orwell's *1984*, in terms of an area of freedom preserved or wrested from the state. Instead, it is conceived as the means by which one individual cuts himself off from others. [...] The withdrawal of an individual was not seen as a form of opposition to the authorities' surveillance but as a kind of moral pathology."[94]

As late as 1977 Roland Barthes, in his lecture at the Collège de France subsequently published under the title *How to Live Together*, still took this idea a step further toward the utopia of a life in completely open space: "Is there such a thing as a model of the anti-hut?" Barthes asks, finding it in Piranesi. The latter's "*Prisons [Carceri]* are supposed to be the anti-hut (note that they are vast, anti-cellular structures, demonic capsizing of levels). Piranesi: 'Out of fear springs pleasure.' That dramatic, criticized breaching of the *quant-à-sois*, that foreclosure of the interiority of the room as a refuge and as a *pleasure* [...] that space of emotional agitation, that ornamental and hysterical transparency: the *magnificenza*."[95]

Robbery and property
Pathology of privacy

Privacy and publicness are discussed primarily in categories of defending a terrain against access by a collective, be it through the state or through other people. The terminology of conflict becomes defining for privacy: private is what must be defended against public or state intrusion.

German law refers to a "right of defense" aimed against being thoroughly spied out by the state or by corporations interested in private data—what Foucault has described as "panopticism," a state in which one has to forever count on being spied out. The reason for this right of defense may lie in historical experiences with totalitarian systems that no longer offered its members any right to privacy or any room for an absolutely inviolable autonomy of action. Yet language, too, defines a negative defensive ideational framework within which our notion of "privacy" takes shape.

The concept of privacy prevalent in Western Europe and America is shaped by an aggressive concept: the Latin word *privare* means "to rob." Being *in privato* thus means being in a space previously wrested from a collective whole, which henceforth needs to be defended against the intrusiveness of the others. Hence, the private sphere is conceived of as robbery and the emergence of property as an act of aggression against the community: one robs something and makes it inaccessible to the others. Only then does it become possible to be *apud se, chez soi*, at home.

This is reinforced by the prevailing notion in Western philosophy that the constitution of the "proper," the self, is an act of distinction from the world. Accordingly, the private is interpreted as an ultimately aggressive act of taking possession of a part of something that originally belonged to all—just like when you parcel an available piece of land and in the process try to get the largest or best parcel, which you subsequently need to defend.

The notion of privacy as a quality that must be eked out and defended is common, yet it is in need of justification and by no means without any alternative. It presupposes a collective origin of mankind. The individual emerges from a multitude of people, draws a circle, perhaps builds a dwelling within it, saying that no one is allowed inside, and defends his "property," his unit against the others.

Japanese architecture points in a different direction. In Fujimoto's "House before House" the rooms drift apart, and nature grows into the hallways and creates new microsquares between the cell-like living spaces. The house is taken apart and, along with it, the arsenal of concepts in which it is thought of.

Here, the private, the capsule to which one retreats, is not something that is partitioned off from common space, as in medieval village communities where a piece of the village green would be split off and declared private. Here, it is the other way around: individual cells are compacted into a collective space that does not lead to the disintegration of those cells. "Public space" develops between the cells.

There is a major theoretical distinction involved here, as the concept of the *privatum* itself predetermines the relationship between individual and community. In a conception where there is initially a collective—say, common land—from which an individual then splits off something that the others can no longer access without permission, the private will invariably have a negative connotation: in the act of privatization the others are excluded.

Another conception would be that the individual came first and only later joined forces with other individuals in a solidary collective: that the private, the individual, the solitary is thus the starting condition of the social game and the individual with his cell goes looking for other cells, only then forming collectives. According to this conception, the private would be something that would occasionally, perhaps, also need to be defended, but not something that was primarily created in an aggressive act aimed against a preexisting collective.

In one instance the collective exists first and the individual defines him or herself in contradistinction to it by "privation" from the common. In the other the individual, as a clearly defined being, forms a community with others. In the first case we are dealing with an act of closing, in the second with one of opening. It would be interesting to examine what this shift in perspective would mean for a theory of property.

Traditional Japanese house with a large roof overhang

Instead of often windowless stone walls with solid wooden doors, such as in ancient Athens, the traditional Japanese house has relatively fragile sliding elements and a terrace-like *engawa*, the roofed transition zone between the interior with tatami mats on the floor and the exterior, which can be added either to one or to the other by means of lightweight sliding room dividers called *shoji*. As a protected space the house shields the occupants vertically, by means of its large, strongly cantilevered roof, from the forces of nature, from intense sun exposure, driving rain, and snow, rather than horizontally from the street space and other people. There is no concept in Japanese that is directly comparable to the Euro-American notion of "privacy"; the loanword "puraibashi" made its way to Japan only at a late point, concurrently with the adoption of Western building and lifestyles.

In Japanese architecture the individual or "private" is thus not defined as an act of "robbery" from collective space, but rather as a prerequisite for the latter. Unlike the classic apartment-sharing community where a single large home is subdivided into private spaces, the new Japanese communal living clusters are composed of cells that are predefined as "private." Moriyama House is just one case in point. It involves a very different concept of privacy and being "at one's own place." For architecture this means composing collective housing of autonomous cells that require sufficient free space even in close association in order to survive as autonomous cells. Specifically, this means that such a mosaic-like composite architecture would need a garden, however small, for each cell, in which one can lie undisturbed in a hammock; a place where one can cook unseen, while a communal kitchen and garden are available for larger parties. Also essential is the possibility of leaving the dwelling unit unseen by other members of the collective.

But why have a private sphere at all? Raymond Geuss mentions three possible reasons aside from the right to physical integrity to protect the private sphere as an area "within which physical or cognitive *access to me* should not be allowed to others not of my choosing":[96] firstly, competitiveness, which allows me to keep information from an opponent that would give him or her an advantage over me; secondly, to be able to perform activities that require a certain degree of concentration; thirdly, because being aware of the presence of others could have an inhibiting effect on the performance of certain activities (cursing, writing letters, sex) that are recognized as constitutive of personality (an achievement of the modern era; in the Middle Ages such activities were usually not accorded a space of their own)—this inhibition would only go away if we were to successfully "change social attitudes […} rather than building up barriers of privacy" (Geuss, p. 93), that is, if we could alter the feeling of disgust and sense of shame in such a way that there would no longer be a need for shielding. What exactly does this mean? It means that if a society has agreed that one does not sleep or have sex in public, the consequence of this agreement is either to build spaces for these activities that are isolated, hidden from view (the "liberal" response, which takes man the way he is) or to think about eliminating the reasons (the "social attitudes") why people are uncomfortable with the idea of having to sleep or have sex in public space (the utopian-paternalistic response).

Aside from the issue of whether this shifting of the boundaries of shame is desirable, the question arises if, and at what civilizational expense, it would be likely—even if in etymological terms, as Geuss delights in mentioning, "the public and the privates (and the public and the pubic) [were] not all that far apart" in antiquity.[97] As long as certain boundaries of disgust and shame are still detectable and socially desired, there is a need for shieldable spaces of privacy.

Architecture of hospitality

And here they take their sweet repast
While house and grounds dissolve
And one by one the guests are cast
Beyond the garden wall
And no one knows where the night is going.
Leonard Cohen, "The Guests"

Geuss and Derrida
Housing and hospitality

Raymond Geuss criticizes "the characteristic modern conception" of privacy where "the individual self-evidently comes first as the autonomous starting point for theorizing and valuation"[98] and community has to find its role in promoting and defending the security and well-being of the individual. Classic liberalism considers the right to isolate oneself from others as a basic prerequisite for individual subjectivity, and leaves it at that. Contrasting with this is the ideal of a society that, even though it does not force its members to give up an autonomous way of life (the ultimate consequence of this would be the terror state), does commit them, beyond the right to retreat, to a form of hospitality and generosity.

The fact that both even need to be called for is a result of the overly successful defense of privacy in the modern era.

The notes of the French author Gilles de Gouberville (1521–1578), who kept a detailed diary of contemporary everyday life in the mid-sixteenth century, document that guests were received in the kitchen and the *salle* at any time of day or night: "No time and no place were reserved exclusively for private life," the historian Madeleine Foisil concludes: "It was not considered an invasion of privacy to enter a man's bedroom at what we would consider an inappropriate hour. In the ordinary course of the day guests who arrived at the manor kitchen close to mealtime were frequently invited to dine."[99] Strangers, in particular, were offered a place to stay for the night: "When the day ended in Mesnil-au-Val ... Gilles de Gouberville would invite his visitor to remain under his protective roof, safe from the dark and the dangers of the night, from the immemorial fear of darkness. Those asked to stay included peasants, villagers, artisans, judges, and noblemen."[100]

One could argue that this role of the house had long been delegated to restaurants and hotels. We must realize, though, to what this outsourcing of vital functions of the house as a place of hospitality and encounter has led: what used to be a place where all of life took place became a cubicle for the nuclear family.

In 1951, Martin Heidegger was invited to give a lecture as part of the Darmstadt Talks organized by the Deutscher Werkbund, an association of artists, architects, designers, and industrialists. Under the title "Building, Dwelling, Thinking," he developed the concept of a "plight of dwelling" that refers not simply to the physical homelessness following the destruction of World War II, but to an existential inability to dwell in terms of being-in-the-world—an argument that can also be read as an attempt by the politically compromised philosopher, whose anti-Semitism becomes obvious not least in his "black notebooks," to move the debate from a political to an anthropological/existential level. "The proper plight of dwelling," as Heidegger writes, "is indeed older than the world wars with their destruction, older also than the increase of the earth's population and the condition of the industrial workers. The proper dwelling plight lies in this, that mortals ever search anew for the essence of dwelling, that they *must ever learn to dwell*. What if man's homelessness consisted in this, that man still does not even think of the proper plight of dwelling as *the* plight?"

To Heidegger, this plight is the result of a misconception of being-in-the-world. Countering the argument that man's original experiences are experiences of security in the cradle, the womb, the lap, the house, and native land, he posits the concept of the "thrownness" of being: that at the onset of being-in-the-world there is the freedom and fear of man having been thrown into an uncanny world. What is placed at the beginning, according to this, is the individual who embarks on a search, rather than the group into which man is born. Even in *Being and Time (Sein und Zeit)* Heidegger had already discussed the illusion of a "natural 'being-at-home'" that brings "man's publicness" into "the average everydayness of being."

To Heidegger, the "space of dwelling" is the exact opposite of its common definition as, say, "something firmly surrounded by walls with a ceiling over one's head and a floor under one's feet."

In *On the Way to Language* (*Unterwegs zur Sprache*) Heidegger reflects in a similar way on a poem by Georg Trakl titled "Winter Evening" (*Winterabend*).

> When the snow falls against the window,
> The evening bell rings long,
> The table is prepared for many,
> And the house is well cultivated.
>
> Some in their wanderings
> Come to the gate on dark paths.
> The tree of grace blooms golden
> From the earth's cool sap.
>
> Wanderer, step silently inside;
> Pain has petrified the threshold.
> There in pure radiance
> Bread and wine glow on the table.
> (Trans. Jim Doss and Werner Schmitt)

Heidegger's main focus is on the enigmatic pain that "petrified the threshold" and that is contrasted with the image of "pure radiance" and a table with bread and wine.

Derrida's paradox of unconditional hospitality

Jacques Derrida addresses the space of hospitality and the paradox of *hospitalité inconditionelle* in a number of texts.

The spaces that interest him are liminal spaces. In *Adieu to Emmanuel Levinas* he raises the question of whether "hospitality [is not] an interruption of the self":[101] what happens when a guest, a stranger, enters the house and is welcomed with the words "Please, feel at home, *comme chez vous*"? The host banks on the guest not taking advantage of the offer, for if he were to take the invitation seriously, he could chase the host out of the house. What would the ethics of unconditional hospitality be? Normally, the relationship between host and guest is necessarily one of subordination. Hospitality is a sovereign's act: in order to offer something to a guest, one needs to own something. Hence hospitality would always be subject to conditions that the guest, the stranger, must respect. The stranger (*xenos*) is only perceived as such as the result of a definition, a pact (*xenia*). A self-definition as citizen or host was always possible only as a result of the appearance of strangers or guests: Socrates was a citizen of Athens, whereas Aristotle, who was born in Stagira, could never become one.[102]

The host asks questions ("Where are you from?") and in doing so turns the other into a stranger. The question is an act of violence, of occupying a terrain. Without this definition, Derrida argues, there would not be any strangers: no *xenos* without *xenia*. Unconditional hospitality would thus be an act that does not take the liberty of asking questions, because it proceeds on the assumption that everyone is fundamentally a stranger.

Être chez soi

One could argue with Derrida that language, too, mirrors doubts about the identity of dwelling and identity. In the German "zuhause sein" (being at home) the preposition *zu* describes a movement toward the *haus*; being in this case is, technically speaking, travel rather than staying put—otherwise the phrase would be "inhause sein." The same applies to "esse apud se" in Latin and "être chez soi" in French, which both mean "being with oneself," and to "being at home" in English: in dwelling, one is only "with oneself," a guest "at oneself," rather than identical with "oneself." The local preposition "at" marks a space, a difference, in which hospitality has its place.

"Hospitality is not simply some region of ethics […] it is ethnicity itself, the whole and the principle of ethics," Derrida writes in *Adieu*:[103] hospitality is culture per se and not one form of ethical

174

behavior among many. The concept of unconditional hospitality lies beyond the terms of law, beyond all rights and obligations. The host must not want to maintain absolute control over his house; the guest must be free of subordination and guilt and cannot be forced to speak in a foreign language, indeed, cannot be made to speak at all.

The notion of dwelling as *être chez soi*, realizing one is a guest "at one's own place," reverses conditions. It implies that only the guest turns the occupant into someone who can open his house and be "at himself." According to this notion, dwelling only becomes possible as a result of knowing about being a guest; the freedom of dwelling would consequently also lie in the symbolic acts of hospitality, in abandoning the construction of self in contradistinction to others and giving up private life for a moment. What emerges here is a different concept of identity that also has implications for architecture.

Inner-city living in the forest, Berlin (Raumlabor, Moritzplatz)

Chapter 7

Shared Spaces

From the Garden City
to the Post-Capitalist Urban Jungle

A square that is a forest

A very different idea of inner-city living was presented by the Berlin-based architecture collective Raumlabor: their proposal involved planting a forest and sowing forest grass on Moritzplatz square in the Kreuzberg neighborhood of Berlin. A large number of small stilt houses would stand, barely recognizable from the ground, among the trees. Thus a forest would be created in the middle of the city that at the same time would be a residential neighborhood and a square. The ground level, the "forest floor," would have remained a space for communal picnics, an adventure playground for children, an open zone devoid of any form of privatization. In this way Raumlabor also points to a basic economic problem of all city debates: the issue of who owns the ground.

In rainy conditions treetops were supposed to offer protection. The idea was that in the middle of the city one would wake up to the sound of rustling branches rather than traffic. Underneath the loosely distributed houses people would stroll, artists would perform, children would chase one another, and during the night foxes would prowl through the undergrowth. It would not be like life in the countryside, but rather like life in the forest, on the reverse side of civilization: the jungle invading the city, where it currently exists only as a tacky metaphor for the big-city feel. Park and architecture, nature and city would be interwoven here; one would no longer be a place of recovery from the other. But what about fire prevention, street (or, rather, field) cleaning? The utopian notion of a communal space with niches of retreat is often countered with the argument that such spaces may be appealing in theory, but tend to fail in practice, when no control is exercised, due to lack of discipline: all it would need for the entire thing to become unusable is for someone to use the cave or a corner of the adventure playground as a toilet— or for two bawling drunks to settle there. An open space can only be kept usable, the argument goes, through constant control and the constant presence of cleaning teams. This may be true in some cases, but can it be generalized?

What a city that defines the space underneath the houses as public and accessible to all could look like, how it could function, and what the relationship of control and openness would be is something that the Lebanese architect and urbanist Youssef Tohme is trying to show in Bordeaux, where he is commissioned to build 4,500 units, 750,000 square feet of office space, and 215,000 square feet of shops on an area of about 150 acres—a new neighborhood called Brazza. On what is a historic floodplain, many of the buildings will be built on stilts, leaving the common ground open to public use. "The district will also retain its working-class identity and more than half of housing units will be classified as social," Tohme explains.

New spaces: strategies of creating form

For architects who want and must invent new squares, new types of housing, and other spaces for a changing society in transformation, the issue of formal principles allowing one to imagine spaces beyond the linguistic and conceptual fetters that architecture has put on itself is essential.

Stacking and digging are the most common ways of creating space. You carve out a monolith, the way Jorge Oteiza does in some of his sculptures, or you pile up materials to create multiple levels, as demonstrated by the structure of Le Corbusier's Maison Dom-Ino.

In art one distinguishes between sculptures that are the result of removing or carving out, that is, of subtracting material (*Skulptur* in German), and such that are created by adding (*Plastik* in German); in architecture one is the cave principle, the other the nest or hut principle.

Yet there are other principles of creating space, such as proliferation (sprawling in space), compression (concentration through compacting), the combination of both, the principle of the thicket, or the principle of siltation familiar from seaside resorts: sand is blown across the streets, creating dunes in the midst of organized space and flowing through the city; in front yards and on parking lots, soft spots appear, small dunes on which children play and where cabdrivers who are waiting for customers rest, as if on a lounger. Recogniz-

Maison Dom-Ino
(Le Corbusier)

179

able forms are inundated and new spaces are created through the dissolution of form.

But how could the principle of the beach, of siltation be transferred into architecture?

Siltation

A university campus is usually organized like a city: there are buildings for the commons, lecture halls, the library, a park in between. The first surprise in Lausanne is that all these functions have their place under the same roof: designed by the Japanese architects SANAA, the 215,000-square-foot Learning Center of the École Polytechnique Fédérale de Lausanne on Lake Geneva is a built dune landscape where everything flows together in a large open continuum of space. From the outside it looks as if gravity has slackened as the result of some weird experiment, allowing the structure to lift off from the ground: the building undulates, creating shaded squares underneath, while a vacillating dune of concrete forms inside.

One enters and walks forever up and down through an open space into which individual uses—a library with half a million books, a cafeteria, lecture halls—are set like islands. It is more than just a dumb joke about Switzerland to point out that the design is reminiscent of two slices of holey cheese that artfully undulate, one on top of the other. The structure forms sometimes small, sometimes large bubbles that serve as courtyards and merge with other bubbles to create an outdoor landscape, while inside one floats through the building as if following the currents in an aquarium. Sometimes the building's glass façade reminds one of an endless film: people go by and reappear, as if having crossed into the realm of fiction, on the other side behind the curving ribbon of glass.

This constant restlessness is both the building's strength and, perhaps, its weakness: whether it is possible to really concentrate on work on those

Rolex Learning Center,
Lausanne (SANAA)

180

islands, in public space and without walls, remains to be seen. In any event this study landscape is a new form of communication architecture: one can lie in small groups on the artificial slopes—as in *The School of Athens*—which is, in fact, encouraged by the omnipresent globular cloth bags drifting like seating floes in the swell of the open space. These bag chairs are, like the concrete waves of the Learning Center, reminiscent of attempts in the 1950s and 1960s to dynamize space: of Oscar Niemeyer's samba Modernism, of Parent's slanted landscaped interiors, and of Eero Saarinen's TWA terminal, whose shape epitomized the joys of taking off, of departure. At the École Polytechnique one is similarly delighted about the structure's metaphorical chargeability—at the opening, reference was made to a system of open nodes, while dim images of neuronal fireworks were being shown to illustrate the point, as if the building were a built brain and we the neurons wildly firing about inside. Still, one does not need to agree at all with this metaphorization of the building to be amazed at its spatial impact. On the one hand, it appears as intimate as a living room with its seating islands and, on the other, as public as a park that is protected from the weather only by thin glass.

Excessive overexposure

The dazzling white that has become a signature of new Japanese architecture plays an important role in these attempts to dissolve concepts of space. Boundaries blur as if one is looking at a world covered by snow—and while Jun'ichiro Tanizaki still celebrated the darkness of traditional Japanese houses in his 1933 "In Praise of Shadows," insisting that Japanese things are at their most beautiful in indeterminate twilight, the opposite applies today: architecture and the things it contains thrive on overexposure to light, which causes spatial boundaries to blur.

The Lausanne Learning Center, which is open every day until midnight, also relies on subtle transitions between spaces; the seat cushion landscape is supposed to develop islands of thought that interlink and float through the waves of the building like intellectual plankton. The somewhat intrusive presence of sponsors in the build-

181

ing—Rolex watches wherever one looks—reminds us that all of this cannot be realized without money. Still, one can sit or lie here and form small or large study groups, and even spontaneous lectures can happen on the ramps. This raises a few practical questions (noise, concentration), yet it draws on the notion of a "university without condition" that Jacques Derrida once called for: a place that invents spaces for "resistance against any form of economic, political, legal, or ethical constraint,"[104] thus becoming a metaphor of a different, more open society. Experimental cultural buildings, even if they are as small as Tobias Rehberger's dazzling Café ARCOmadrid, were—and still are—such places of counterpublicness (that is why they are so important in times of crisis): places where a society reflects on itself in a different way. And it is not surprising that SANAA's landscaped collective-living-room-like study facility is strongly reminiscent of Constant Nieuwenhuys's "post-revolutionary," "anti-capitalist" city of "New Babylon," a utopian project for a city in which there are no longer any public and private spaces and the division of buildings and areas of life into "work" and "family" no longer exists. Because work is fully automatized and private property has been abolished, the resident of New Babylon, freed of wage labor, roams across the plateaus of a metabolic megastructure that is suspended above the old cities with their single-family homes and factories and other tribulations, like *Homo Ludens* looking for sensuous experiences and new adventures: he eats, sleeps, and meets people wherever he wants.

In Orbit, Düsseldorf
(Tomás Saraceno)

The Dutch artist, musician, author, and architect Constant Nieuwenhuys (1920–2005), who conceived this hedonistic urban structure between 1959 and 1974, was a member of the Situationist International, a leftist association of European artists established in 1957. In addition to the abolition of wage labor and any social hierarchies, the Situationists called for the creation of conditions that would allow new ways of human togetherness, conditions in which life itself would become an artwork. Architecture was supposed to provide the framework for such conditions.[105]

"This revolution could become just as momentous as the first French Revolution," the French artist Nicolas Schöffer wrote about May 1968. Under the impression of the revolt he published his overheated, sweeping utopian proposal *La ville cybernétique* the following year.[106] In Schöffer's weird redesigned world, which is supposed to "demediocritize" life, there are large buildings that accommodate up to 30,000 people and multiple prisms with colorful light projections, in which bodies are uncoupled from normal categories of time and space and float around like in a trip. The residences are suspended on concrete piers between thirty and one hundred feet above the ground, which belongs to everyone—in this, Schöffer's is an early precursor of the utopian design of the Berlin Raumlabor collective. Artificial fragrances are supposed to relax the resident. One of the central large buildings is a bulbous tower with an ascending spiral ramp that looks like a swollen Guggenheim Museum. It houses the "Center for Sexual Leisure Activities," a "temple of love" where there is "no tendency whatsoever toward pornography," but rather "an audiovisual bath with a mildly warm, fragrant atmosphere, curvaceous forms of smooth material that are moderately warm to the touch," as well as forms "that make a slowly pulsating movement and are meant to evoke a sense of swelling": artificial plants in a built landscape of emotions that "prepares couples for sexual love, which then will finally be demystified, accessible to all, unaffected, and no longer demeaned." "On the way toward humans who

New Babylon (draft),
(Constant Nieuwenhuys)
Café ARCOmadrid, Madrid
(Tobias Rehberger)

are free from all false constraints," these centers would "fulfill a social task of immense importance."[107] In Schöffer's case the collective architectural vision is a state of sustained orgy and the city of the future a gigantic, relaxed love machine; an echo of these utopian designs can still be heard today in the large-scale installations of the Argentinian artist Tomás Saraceno, a trained architect: there, too, one hovers through space in interconnected bubbles, except that this utopian public-dwelling project is now only possible in the preserve of the museum, under the label of art.

Nested-in shop, Rome

Chapter 8

Closed and Open Systems

Architecture as sculpture
The tragic modern super-sign

While contemporary art moves closer and closer to experimental architectures in formal terms, the star system of international architecture produces ever more art objects.

Many of the signature buildings with which architects such as Zaha Hadid and Sir Norman Foster cover the world follow space-ship logic. What is inside and what is outside is clear, just as it is clear—and essential to know—what is inside and what is outside in a spaceship: inside is where there is air to breathe, outside is the

Lotus, Venice Biennale
(Zaha Hadid)

other. Spaceship logic defines the outside as a hostile zone. Perhaps the success of space-ship buildings has something to do with the previously discussed shift in how people relate to public space, which was a promise that has become a problem, a space that is primarily characterized by rituals of control and efficiency enhancement.

Yet art, too, has such hypertrophic super-signs that similarly shape and define public space. Anish Kapoor's *Cloud Gate*, for instance, is a gigantic sculpture that from a distance looks like a chrome-plated giant bean. Created in 2004, the 100-ton, 23-million-dollar work is one of the attractions of Chicago's Millennium Park, a pub-

lic park sponsored by major corporations and located next to a business district, where, in addition to Kapoor's *Cloud Gate*, one can visit a pedestrian bridge designed by Frank Gehry and funded by the oil company BP, and the McDonald's-sponsored Cycle Center; the money for Kapoor's work was provided by AT&T.

The collection of these sculptures, and Kapoor's *Cloud Gate* in particular, reflects a change in what is expected of public art. Richard Serra was commissioned by communities and public institutions in the 1970s and the slabs of steel he put up were celebrated for cutting through and disrupting public space, thereby enabling new experiences of space. These sculptures stood for the far-reaching hopes of a critical theory of public or architectural art: large-scale sculptures were to turn the user of a square into a more alert, critical, and active actor on the stage of the city.

With Anish Kapoor this hope has been turned into the opposite. Scaled down, Kapoor's *Cloud Gate* could also serve as a hand-friendly paperweight or a novel perfume bottle. Public space is adorned with gently decorative objects, as if it were shopwindow decoration. Rather than being the stage of active citizenship, it adopts the formal principle of appealing product presentation; what takes center stage is the consumer object, rather than action, with those who live in the city standing passively and wide-eyed in front of it. The art object is, in this case, a monumental signet that primarily demonstrates the power of private agents in public space: it defines the city's public space as a museum. It is a hermetic, exclusive object that can be viewed, but not appropriated, lived in, accessed, or taken over.

Cloud Gate, Chicago
(Anish Kapoor)

The city as image: Celebration

Examples of a different, exclusive kind of image-production, of closed systems, are the residential towns of New Urbanism. The most famous of these, Celebration, a town for 11,000 residents located south of Orlando, Florida, looks like an awfully idyllic and typical American small town that has evolved over many decades. Yet nothing has simply evolved here: the city is the result of the largest market research analysis ever to address town planning in America.

In the 1960s, the Disney Company actually wanted to build something very different here: under a gigantic glass bubble, bullet trains were to thunder into a fully air-conditioned city center; jet fighters were to swoosh past skyscrapers and the design for the houses resembled habitable remote controls in which robots with glowing eyes ministered to the occupants. "Progress City" was a

Celebration, Orlando, Florida

design by Herb Ryman, one of Walt Disney's "imagineers" who worked on the "experimental prototype community of tomorrow," the final and most ambitious project of the company's founder. Epcot was to become a model for a new American urbanism. When Disney died, the project was disregarded and the urban utopia degenerated into a theme park. The company founder's plans were only taken up again by Disney CEO Michael Eisner. In 1996, his American town of the future became a reality, except that very little in it is reminiscent of the present: the residences have white porches, muntin windows, and fake dormers that are delivered in large cardboard boxes and screwed onto the roofs. The town has an artificial lake and a boardwalk with rocking chairs and cafés in the center, a Main Street, and a few small stores where dapper employees sell nostalgic products; everything is homemade, locally grown.

Celebration is primarily a result of lifestyle research performed by the Disney Company. The company commissioned the Stanford Research Institute to establish the average American's idea of an ideal town. That ideal town, it turned out, is situated on a small lake with a park, and has a city hall and a Main Street with shops and restaurants; it has no unemployed people and no highways. The ideal house has muntin windows, bays, and a front yard, and on Sundays one sits with the family on the porch or by the fireplace. When you stroll in the subtropical early-morning haze past César Pelli's small-town movie theater, you hear nothing but the gurgling of the lake and the sound of golf balls being hit. Not much was left to chance: anyone wanting to build in Celebration had to order one of several types of prefab houses, for which Disney offered various historical façade styles from the stock of national history: "classical," "Victorian," "colonial revival," "coastal," "French," and "Mediterranean," as well as "craftsman."

Only at second glance does one realize that this idyll, which seems to be set openly into the landscape, also has fortifications that are as invisible as they are impossible to overcome: the center of Celebration is semisurrounded by an artificial lake, while the golf course extends on the other side. Anyone who wants to leave Celebration has to either drive across a small arched bridge or down Campus Street, which cuts across the golf course. Hence anyone wanting to steal a TV has to either row across the lake or run across the golf course. The lake and golf course thus form a subtle line of defense and the idea to have the golf course lit at night is not just a service for the well-off middle class who have taken up residence here, but also a security-related move that unnoticeably turns the sports grounds into a border strip: a fortress in the guise of an open landscape idyll.

"It's the town you want to call home," the promotional brochure proclaims, and everything in Celebration bespeaks stasis, comfort, and security. Even the car, once proudly parked in the front yard as a fetish of boundless freedom, is banished from view: garages are to be built behind the homes; there is no front lawn with driveway, just porches, the Tom Sawyer and Gatsby kind of wooden porches that shape the mythical image of the American home. Disney's social utopia managers coined a new word for what is supposed to happen there: "front-porch friendliness."[108] You are supposed to sit on the porch, chat with the neighbors, and offer a brownie to the children riding by on bicycles. Social proximity is pledged with your signature under the purchase contract. Celebration thus appears like a rehearsal camp for lost small-town solidarity and neighborliness. Front-porch friendliness belongs to Celebration like the bicycle, which has become a symbol of the new upper class and

Plan view, Celebration

191

Types of houses,
Celebration

features, as a promise of happiness, in the town's logo: those who take a leisurely bike ride in the morning to the boardwalk café have left the world of social acceleration pressures behind them.

Ryman's EPCOT was an expansion fantasy. The ideal cities of Modernism share traits with Christian eschatology; like in the Book of Revelation, the new paradise was not a garden but an elusive metropolis, the heavenly Jerusalem. The subtext of Disney's ideal town, on the other hand, promises a return to paradise—one that to many, indeed, seemed like paradise—that is, until Matteo Giovanditto appeared.

Murder in Celebration

The neighbors didn't know much about him. They knew that he used to live in Massachusetts and they knew he had a Chihuahua and a black Corvette he always parked in the same place. In late November 2010 the neighbors started to get worried: the Corvette was not standing where it always stood and Giovanditto had not walked the dog in days—two facts that in any other city would not have been cause for anyone seriously to worry, but that here, in Celebration, prompted the neighbors to call the police. And, indeed, the 58-year-old Giovanditto was found murdered in his home: on Thanksgiving he had been attacked with an ax and subsequently strangled with a shoelace.

According to FBI statistics, about 14,000 people are murdered every year in the United States, which is an average of about 38 people a day[109]—but this was the first time since 1994, when Celebration was founded, that a murder had happened there. Yet it was not the first time that the other, dark world had penetrated the décor here: the case merely uncovered the hidden darkness inside the sealed-off utopia.

David-Israel Murillo was 28 when he murdered Giovanditto and was convicted of the crime two years later. He explained in court that Giovanditto had offered him money to wash his sports car and had given him beer that was allegedly laced with sleep-inducing drugs. When he woke up, he found Giovanditto on top of him, attempting to sexually assault him. Murillo then found the ax, hit him several times, and strangled him with the shoelace to make sure that Giovanditto was dead.[110]

Murillo, who claimed he had never attended school and had lived for years at a homeless shelter, had sustained himself with odds jobs ever since he had lost his job at a bakery. Yet the army of job seekers, gardeners, cleaning ladies, and laborers like Murillo were not the first, after all, to bring the reality of the outside world into Celebration. Shortly afterwards, two journalists, Barbara Spindel and Maria Elena Fernandez, shocked the people of Celebration with an article that revealed the truth about the victim: before moving to Celebration, Giovanditto was said to have worked as a teacher under a different name and sexually abused students. The artificial idyll of Celebration had apparently made the town also particularly attractive to all those whom the residents thought they were safe from.

A theory of nidation
The informal city

Informal urbanism constitutes a countermovement to the super-sign architecture and zombified city-image production that has developed in recent years. It defines architecture not as an object, but rather as an open framework that allows embedments of all kinds and thus generates a different concept of housing.

Architectures beyond inside and outside
The Yokohama Apartments

In Japan, the new interest in fundamentally reorganizing the private and the public beyond issues of isolation or seclusion is resulting in spaces that cannot be assigned to a particular typology: this space could just as easily be a living room as part of the street, a square with a kitchen, or a kitchen without walls. The architecture firm On Design demonstrates this with its Yokohama Apartments, where several stair towers lead from a loggia that is open to the street to the four apartments above. The latter are furnished with a bathroom and a kitchenette, so that the occupants do not have to show up in the communal kitchen at times when they want to eat something but prefer not to see anyone. The autonomous core cells of privacy, which did not exist in this form in apartment-sharing communities, hang like treetops over an open ground-floor area that is the site of communal life. This is where parties and exhibitions take place (several of the occupants are artists) and what happens is something that, within the categories of European concepts of the city and housing, was inconceivable except as a surrealist anxiety dream: street and living space become one; the room grows into the city. Coming from Europe, where popular discourse about public squares is limited to the issue of how to cope with acts of violence and vandalism, one is amazed that this openness is not abused. Often a festive mood emerges, a sense of community that is anything but compulsive and which is remotely reminiscent of the long communal tables in old Italian mountain villages—or of the dinner parties of antiquity, the *convivia*, which were a public affair. The Yokohama Apartments reinvent the kitchen as an actual semipublic *piazzetta* that can only be closed provisionally with transparent curtains.

Yokohama Apartment,
Kanagawa (ON design partners)

The open city
Ideological dogmatism of building policies: the case of the failed Werkbund housing estate in Munich

Why has similarly experimental collective architecture—for which, as we have seen, a number of examples exist—not yet been attempted on the scale of an entire city district? The answer lies in the narrow-mindedness of clearly identifiable policymakers, in Munich, for instance. A few years ago, the local Werkbund organization (an association of artists, architects, designers, and industrialists) developed a plan for an experimental city district—but made the mistake of committing to particular builders at the time of the competition: in this case, tested, extremely conservative, and timid municipal housing associations, whose representatives could not even imagine creating bedrooms above a common area, so as to save dead hallway space.

Nevertheless—and in the spirit of the Werkbund's pioneering Weissenhof estate in Stuttgart, which had been conceived by Mies van der Rohe and others in 1927 as an experimental laboratory of lifestyles and housing forms for a new democratic society—the Munich Werkbund wanted to build five hundred homes on the site of former military barracks, one half privately financed, the other publicly funded, that were to show what the city of the twenty-first century could look like. A jury selected the plans of the Japanese architect Kazunari Sakamoto.

Sakamoto designed a masterpiece of Asian compaction, a forest of small towers with hanging gardens, loggias, and green roofs, a modern San Gimignano, a miniature Tokyo for Munich. Paths, small squares, and private gardens hidden from view by tall hedges were haphazardly distributed between the houses; there were areas that looked like rural idylls and others that were spacious and big-city-like; there was student housing and housing for the elderly, luxury lofts, and public roof gardens that promised the residents a view of the Alps. And to show that education and integration were to play a greater role, the center of the estate was not a so-called piazza, but rather a kindergarten with swimming pool. It was not a coincidence that Sakamoto wanted to put a kindergarten, an adventure landscape in the center of his Werkbund world: a place where shared adventures happen, where caves are built and games are played, where communal life is tried out. This image of the city as a place of shared adventures serves as a contrast to life in the isolated nuclear family in the heavily mortgaged suburban home.

Werkbund Siedlung in Munich, model (Kazunari Sakamoto)

It would have become a sensation, a social, aesthetic, and ecological one. For if the builders and the city had worked together on this design, the housing estate would have shown that what people look for in the countryside is quite compatible with the city as well: a garden of one's own, tranquility, intimacy, a view of nature—and, on the other hand, a new form of neighborly closeness. Ultimately, this attractiveness is the only ecological argument in the proper sense: only affordable and appealing urban architecture can prevent a daily stream of commuters pouring into the countryside. Looked at in this light, the argument of the Green Party (a coalition partner in the local government), that the small towers were less ecological than the usual blocks because of their larger exterior surface, is dogmatic nonsense. If something had been built that would have kept people from moving to the suburbanized villages, it would most certainly have been an ecological gain, considering the quantities of exhaust gas that suburban commuters blow into the atmosphere every year.

The city as reef
Life in the raised basement

A "raised basement" is not the same
as a ground floor. On a ground floor
everything is planned down to the
last detail: the entrance here, a shop
window there, a shop here. A raised
basement exists primarily because a
building has been raised and it usually has only small openings that provide access to utility and basement
spaces.

Taking a closer look at the raised
basements of old Italian *palazzi*, one
can discover something of an early
model of inclusive urbanism in the
way they were used. These raised
basements are by no means for-
tresses: most of them are porous and

Superstructure of the
Teatro di Marcello, Rome
Car repair, Rome

form niches, small nooks. Demolished in the 1930s, the Palazzo
Caprini, Bramante's first secular building in Rome, had a rusticated
raised basement which accommodated shops—a form that Bramante adopted from classical architecture, where a great number of
shops could embed themselves underneath the living quarters.

The raised basement was thus not a distancing form, but rather a
porous, permeable zone where public life spilled into the house.
Similar configurations from the sixteenth century can be found at the
Palazzo Caffarelli Vidoni and the Palazzo Alberini Cicciaporci. At
the same time, the raised basement is always the site of a jump in
scale, where the monumental order frays into the mundane and
small-scale: at the Palazzo Capranica a tiny restaurant with green
blinds embeds itself into the raised basement, and in Milan, where
the Galleria Vittorio Emanuele II ends in the Piazza della Scala, a
tiny newspaper shop docks onto the monumental form. Bars, kiosks,
even small supermarkets settle in the raised basements of Italian
palazzi like barnacles, and the streets in front of them are, with just a

Galleria Vittorio
Emanuele II, Milan

few gestures, a couple of chairs and tables, defined as places to linger and relax: that which embedded itself—the café—in turn expands into the city.

The raised basement here is an urban zone, where permeability, openness, and concentration create an architecture of hospitality: the house hosts the city with its parasitic microorganisms and both benefit from it. When discussing the raised basement as a porous, inclusive, open, undefined form, we could see it not just as a picturesque nostalgic phenomenon of old Italian town centers, but also as a model—not by rebuilding it in formal terms, but rather by taking it as a figure of thought, as a structural inspiration for a different kind of spatiality.

Many ground floors of contemporary architecture do not allow for any embedment and life slips off them. The countermodel to this would be a house that is lowered into the city like an artificial reef and whose raised basement, rather than serving to distance and reject, offers a deep surface that allows ever new forms of urban life to embed themselves in it or dock onto it, such as barnacles, clams, and sponges. A similar process could be observed in the palace of the Roman emperor Diocletian. Built from AD 295 until 305 in present-day Split in Croatia, the structure occupied a surface of 323,000 square feet. Over the centuries the city ate its way beyond the palace walls, shops embedded themselves, residences were created from disintegrating buildings, houses settled on the cross street, and today the palace, the huge residence of the emperor, has become a city for many with countless small alleys; the residence was overwritten by the city.

Arno Brandlhuber's Brunnenstrasse House

In Europe, architecture is emerging that converts unfinished and abandoned buildings with modest means—especially in Berlin. For years there was an unfinished spec building at Brunnenstrasse in Berlin that had water standing in the basement. The architect Arno Brandlhuber continued construction of the spec building in the most inexpensive way possible: the concrete was finished with so-called smoothing machines, which obviated the need for cement flooring and saved money; instead of an elaborate façade, the concrete skeleton was faced with inexpensive polycarbonate boards, which have astonishing thermal insulation qualities and, moreover, create a surprising visual effect: in sunlight the building glistens, as if it were covered by a film of oil, in shades ranging from pink to green, and at night it shimmers like a subtle Japanese screen. Brandlhuber even manages to wrest a distinctive aesthetic from home improvement store staples; in his hands even a chain-link fence serving as stair railing looks minimalistically noble. Everything is plain,

Brunnenstrasse
House, Berlin
(Arno Brandlhuber)

cheap, and has a raw beauty that is reminiscent of Latin-American improvisational Modernism—the house is an open shelf into which all kinds of things can embed themselves. Toward the side of the interior courtyard, the roof above the top floors folds into an abstracted, walkable mountain hillside that has a tree growing on it. Because construction costs were kept under 92 euros per square foot, Brandlhuber is able to rent the spaces inexpensively to people who otherwise could not afford comparable offices in this location—the ground floor, for instance, to young art dealers. In social terms, too, the building honors the laboratory quality that its form visually promises.

Guerilla urbanism
Raumlabor's Kitchen Monument

But does a place where one can linger and relax even have to be created by means of fixed structures? Or could one imagine a mobile structure that temporarily embeds itself somewhere and creates space wherever it appears?

A simple example of such "urban generators" are the urban beaches; another would be the Kitchen Monument, developed by the Berlin-based architecture collective Raumlabor together with the specialists of Plastique Fantastique for the Akzente cultural festival in the Ruhr region: excess pressure causes a transparent bubble to unfold from a container, a bubble that can be accessed through an airlock and that is big enough for up to eighty people to eat or dance in it.

The container was initially installed as a sculpture in forbidding places, such as underneath a highway overpass or in a desolate park: you simply blow the pneumatic monument into the city like chewing gum. Due to its shape it does not compete with the existing environment, but rather wraps around trees, pillars, and buildings, only to disappear again without leaving any marks.

The membrane creates an open, weather-protected, mobile intermediate space that travels through the city and is put to ever new uses. Raumlabor draws on the tradition of ephemeral baroque festive architecture, as well as on Buckminster Fuller, Yona Friedman, and Archigram, and offers a proposal as to how the city as a civilization model can be helped to recover from increasing social segrega-

Kitchen Monument
(Raumlabor)

tion. A utopian spirit of bricolage informs this project, a new conception of what architecture can be—that is, not static, built for eternity, inflexible, and expensive, but rather demountable, mobile, and a stage that is as open as possible for all kinds of uses. Implied in this is a political deconstruction of the systems that shape building practice and city planning: who decides how public space is configured, how people build, with what materials and in what forms? Who has an interest in public space looking the way it does—and how can those systems, if necessary, be defined down or circumvented? All these questions are raised by the "Pneumament," which can, in fact, not only be used as a mobile restaurant, but also as a temporary shelter, as the plainest form of housing: as a membrane that separates the sleeping place from the surrounding world.

Living at the edge
Housing for those who can't afford architecture

Nowhere is the relationship of nature and city as neatly arranged as in Manhattan: from Staten Island you see the stalagmites of the high-rises, the most intense concentration of architecture surrounded by the relative emptiness of the Hudson and the East River: an image of emptiness versus one of overcrowding. And then, in the center of Manhattan, nature: as if served on a plate in the rectangle of Central Park, again surrounded by four walls of high-rises, the green courtyard of Manhattan.

In the metropolises of the twenty-first century, in Asia and Latin America, this is different: the jungle principle, the confusing interpenetration and superimposition of wasteland, multilevel highways, high-rises, slums, exotic vegetation, neon signs, warehouses, luxury, older buildings, and weathered ruins of modern functional architecture dominates the picture; buildings and nature form an inextricable thicket.

Pushing into this thicket are hundreds of millions of people who in the coming years and decades will have to work and be accommodated in those metropolitan areas.

But how is this feasible? Even subviding the types of settlement appearing on the outskirts and in the midst of the metropolises into illegal slums and official city planning no longer works. In Buenos Aires there is Villa 24, a slum whose streets do not appear on any map of the city, yet the infrastructure is better organized there than in many of the official social housing projects, such as Barrio Soldati, a public housing development that was completed in 1978. In Brazil,

201

too, the favelas are by now barely distinguishable from city districts that have grown organically.[111] Heliópolis in the southeast area of São Paulo was, in the 1970s, originally a favela; today more than 100,000 people live there, the muddy tracks have been paved and are now official streets. The favela Rio das Pedras in the eastern part of Rio de Janeiro has by now developed into a center in its own right. Processes of gentrification can be observed in slums, too: houses are expanded, shops pop up, and the poorest of the poor are relegated to the edges of the slums, where they live in makeshift shelters.

These transformation processes are interesting to observe for urbanists and housing researchers—but they are also potentially dangerous.

The Torre David

The Torre David was actually supposed to be called Centro Financiero Confinanzas and to become the headquarters of a Venezuelan bank. In 1994, construction was halted in the wake of a financial crisis, and from then on the 48-story tower was vacant until, in 2007, slum dwellers started to move into the half-finished concrete rack. Today, 750 families live there in an "informal society." Using ordinary bricks, they have built houses and apartments for themselves into the concrete grid of the building's levels; some of the floors have been lovingly tiled.

A bunch of moped riders chauffeur occupants with their purchases as far up the parking garage ramps as possible to the desired

Torre David, Caracas

level. The architects Alfredo Brillembourg and Hubert Klumpner have documented these structures and are developing models in Caracas for converting vacant parking garages into residential buildings in similar ways. In one of his texts, the critic and curator Justin McGuirk—who, together with the Urban Think Tank team of architects, won the Golden Lion for Best Project at the 2012

Venice Biennale of Architecture for their presentation of the Torre David—raises the question of what happens "when all the speculative buildings in the high-rise sector serve no discernible purpose, other than to add to a speculative bubble."[112] His answer: the Torre David could also serve as a model for converting the super-signs of a flawed capitalism into residential buildings and vertical villages.

The Torre David project has ever since been celebrated as a successful example of "urbanism from below." Formally, on a technical, system-theory level, what is happening there is indeed interesting: the super-sign of a bank becomes a vertical city, a framework into which new usages can be incorporated, docked, or rebuilt. But, unfortunately, that is only half the story.

Misery as picturesque: the new favela chic

What could a real political turnaround of construction and housing in slums look like?

In recent years the favela has become a favorite subject of news coverage and architecture workshops, especially in Europe. Studies have been devoted to how people in need help themselves, how they build structures, and how, ultimately, a functioning microstructure with small stores, workshops, and small squares develops. In much the same way that the affluent twentieth-century visitor to Italy would be touched by the sight of a small Sicilian village and take out his camera to photograph the children and the picturesquely seedy houses, the European of today stands before the favela, delighting in the details of its structures—and forgetting that these, too, are the result of hardship: houses become smaller where people do not have cranes and backhoes at their disposal. And so the favela is celebrated as the return of the sadly missed old European city with its alleys and leaning small houses.

By now, all of the major Latin-American cities offer favela tours, after which tourists leave the slums feeling good that the poor people, too, have somehow managed to make things nice for themselves. In travel brochures, favela tours appear between swimming with dolphins and extreme rock-climbing tours, and the website of the Rio de Janeiro-based agency Adventure Tours lists the favela tour as an "ultimate experience" between "extreme sports" and "hiking." Watching poor people build and dwell becomes another option next to diving excursions with reef sharks, while both are advertised by referring to the appeal of the moderately dangerous.

Picturesque Italy: Portofino
Latin-American favela

The emotional, middle-class view of the favelas, of the beauty and the inventiveness of the poor who populate, say, the ruin of the Torre David in Caracas, soon ends in depoliticized kitsch. It blocks out the insufferableness of life there; it overlooks the fact that at the Torre David women are beaten up, people are hunted down and blackmailed, that the favelas are often ruled by clans who have developed a paramilitary protection system and a realtor system of their own that earns a few players a lot of money and engulfs many residents in even greater misery. The romantic view of the favelas delegates the organization of life in these hells, with an attitude of "it works, after all," to those who have ended up there. References to the ingenious self-organization in the favelas often have a neoliberal coldness about them that one finds at charity events organized by the very people who are, in fact, responsible for the misfortune of the poor, which they now graciously mitigate through fundraising.

According to a study by UN-Habitat, more than thirty percent of all city dwellers will live in slums in the coming two decades, and the trend is rising.[113] A society that continues to cherish the idea of a dignified and anxiety-free life has to start here, with this development, which has both a political and an architectural dimension: working conditions have to be defined in such a way that earned income allows for a dignified life. According to statistics of the NGO "A roof for my country"[114] (*Un Techo para mi País*, UTPMP), about half a million people in Buenos Aires live in slums, more than half of which have been built on public land, and half of that under or next to highways and close to landfills. More than eighty percent do not have sewerage or gas supply. There are elementary schools in these slums, but no secondary schools, which is one reason why the level of education is low and there is practically no opportunity for social mobility—except maybe by illegal means.

There are political options to improve this situation: one could build sewage systems and schools, and landfills could be moved. A policy dealing with what among architects is called, almost too nonchalantly, "slum upgrading"[115] (as if the slum dweller were an air traveler whom the government has kindly upgraded from "homeless" to "tin shack without toilet—not bad, considering!") cannot confine itself to springing for a fountain here and a little tarmac there. It has to develop a plan that goes further than just slightly improving the existing, self-built infrastructure.

This question still receives far too little attention in architecture departments: what could construction look like that goes beyond cosmetic "slum upgrades"? Some architecture schools and projects are pointing the way in this regard. In 2007, two young Ecuadorian architects, Pascual Gangotena and David Barragán, founded the firm Al Borde, which passes on architectural and structural knowhow to poor people who cannot afford an architect, thereby contributing to a no-budget building culture.

In São Paulo in the 1970s, a multilevel concrete block went up that was never completed. For years the concrete skeleton on Rua Sólon stood empty until, in the 1980s, homeless families started to squat the building and create makeshift dwellings for themselves there, with home-made sanitary installations and exposed power lines. In spite of the precarious housing situation the building was popular: there are many job opportunities, schools, and welfare facilities nearby. In 2002, students of the Architecture and Urbanism College at the University of São Paulo, along with the seventy-three families living in the building, began to clean up the property,[116] install a common electricity network, and paint the façade. The façade received the lettering "Edifício União," in order to give the building a face. Gates were installed at both ends of the small alley in front of the building to create a small, elongated courtyard where the children can safely play. Additional steps involve creating a common roof terrace on the flat roof and converting the depressing, small hole of an entrance into a stately lobby, a kind of public living room, where one can sit with visitors. Plans also include a library, where tutoring will be offered and lectures held, and a meeting room for the occupants. The roof terrace would lend itself to common barbecue evenings and would give the occupants a sense that they do not just have a roof over their heads but, in fact, live at a special place. With just a few interventions the character of the complex had already improved somewhat.

Yet in a way, the mistakes of the housing projects of the 1970s repeat themselves when dealing with the favelas: evolved structures are torn down and replaced with drawing board visions. The result is a loss of quality of life. The open spaces that sometimes serve as playgrounds, sometimes as meeting rooms, the narrow streets where people meet: everything that the small-scale patchwork quality of the favela offered is gone here. The occupants are robbed of the last asset they still had: proximity to the others.

The favela should not be romanticized. One can alter and improve it, create jobs, build schools and markets in its midst, create roof gardens for vegetable growing and lay out gardens where currently garbage is piling up—just as empty parking lots in Detroit are, as part of the frequently described movement to reclaim the city, being turned into "urban farms" and people jointly grow vegetables where old Pontiacs used to rust away.[117]

Design proposal for an open urban structure (Christian Esteban Calle Figueroa)

Remaining on site: a new role for the architect

And as a planner one can think the chaotic informal city further in an improved form. A model has been developed under Marc Angélil at the ETH Zürich: students attending a seminar on favelas proposed expanding the favela by adding a city of empty concrete frames with power and water supply that, in consultation with the city, can be settled by the residents and enlarged according to their needs. A space that is open to the street would be turned into a shop or a public kitchen or, alternatively, into a start-up office. The structure allows for narrow towers to be added when living space is needed. Of course, such open urbanism only functions when other framework conditions are created as well: if the young, small-scale start-up entrepreneur gets a microcredit for his office and if the land does not fall prey to land speculation. Such government guidance as encouragement of initiatives has, contrary to the constant complaints of some liberals, nothing to do with the old social paternalism of the welfare state. Instead it is not just an ethical social investment, but also one that makes economic sense: if one can transform favelas into thriving microeconomies, the huge social consequential costs associated with slumification and pauperization of the residents can be avoided.

Underlying both approaches are completely different conceptions of housing: on the one hand, people are provided with a finished home which they then have to deal with themselves, whereas on the other hand, an open space is created that fills up over the years, that can be adapted, redefined, and that can transform itself without any further guidance by architects—as prefigured in 1964 by Bernard Rudofsky in his legendary book *Architecture without Architects* and by Giancarlo de Carlo in his 1970 essay *Architecture's Public*. In one case the residents are occupants of a concept that was concocted somewhere else; the antithesis to this is the occupant as agent, as active codesigner of his neighborhood and his city.

This redefinition also applies to the architect, who becomes an initiator and attendant of social processes without necessarily standing on the side of power and capital.

The Colony: models for new communal spaces

In the context of preparations for the exhibition *Expo 1 – Ecology* at MoMa PS1 in New York in the summer of 2013, the question arose as to where to put up the artists, writers, musicians, architects, and students who, during the large-scale exhibition, were to study and discuss new ways of dealing with ecological and social issues in one-week seminars and workshops, and where they would be able to present their work. The idea came up to build a temporary structure in the outdoor courtyard of PS1 for the duration of the exhibition— a model for a new form of communal life and collective work, of privacy and publicness under precarious conditions, and at the same time a redefined exhibition format.

The first plan was to construct a plain wooden structure like a shelf against the tall concrete wall of the courtyard, a scaffolding-like structure with three levels.[118] Small and simple dwelling units were to be created on the top two levels—freestanding hotel rooms, as it were, in which the participants would live. That the occupants were not permanently exposed to public view would be guaranteed not just by the museum's opening hours, but also by a buffer zone of densely growing plants that would serve both as a garden for the community and as a privacy shield. Instead of signs saying "private" to keep the public from climbing up, the thicket of plants was to create a jungle-like maze that did not separate the intimate from the common space with just a single cut, but functioned like a green filter between the two spheres. The threshold here would be a maze behind which one felt protected rather than walled in. The areas between the box-like dwellings were left to the occupants; there, people could hang hammocks, grow vegetables, put chairs or kiddie pools, and, in individual cases, build additions to their personal cells.

The upper levels would have been two villages of freestanding hotel rooms stacked one on top of the other, with the individual "rooms" separated by small open spaces or gardens. These open spaces distinguished the project substantially from the way apartment buildings are normally constructed. While the latter glues together apartments to create the maximum amount of living space, the Colony was to reduce the individual dwelling units on the same floor area to the absolute minimum of intimate space (bed, small

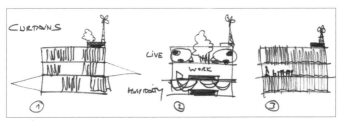

Draft for the Colony at MoMA PS1

table, kitchenette, shower and toilet) and instead enlarge the balcony to room or garden size.

The lower floor was to include, in a space delineated only by curtains, a collective kitchen with a long table that was to also be open to visitors. Lectures, film screenings, and workshops were to take place there. Depending on their needs, the occupants of the structure could use the curtains to create more intimate or more open spaces.

Eventually, the Argentinian architectural firm A77 was awarded the building contract for the Colony. They constructed it in the form of scaffolding; the dwelling units were replaced with camping trailers and tents that ended up being installed behind the structure, because for safety reasons only a single trailer was allowed on the scaffolding. In order to keep costs down, collective showers and toilets had to be built, so that two essential elements of the original design were dropped.

The open space of the ground floor functioned, though: guests came almost every day; lectures and performances took place; visitors mingled with the occupants; anyone was allowed to watch, participate, and join the discussion. In its basic design the Colony was a laboratory for a new architecture of hospitality, a model test to determine how much personal space a human being needs and in what places community can take what forms—how to relate the intimate and the collective in a different way, separate them by means of other filters, and bring them together again in hybrid spaces such as the large, open kitchen on the ground floor—a new form that is a cross between public square and collective living room.

The Colony, at MoMA PS1,
New York, 2013

The house was no longer architecture in the traditional sense: it consisted of that which is erected before construction—scaffolding—and that which is installed after construction in order to control light and the need for protection—curtains. It was built with what comes before and after building. It was no longer separated from its surroundings by walls and no longer opened by means of doors: it functioned more like a sponge that lets the outside world in and in which small encapsulations and a thicket of plants and objects protect the intimacy of its occupants.

An optimized version is the "Berlin Colony,"[119] which is to be put up in Berlin in the summer of 2016. Several towers contain spaces that can be used for sleeping, as well as kitchens and bathrooms. Spaces can be combined vertically to allow larger groups to live there, with occupants each having their own bathroom and toilet unit. In the center these towers are connected by various gardens: a lawn for sunbathing, a field, a kitchen garden, a kind of extended living room under trees. In this case, too, both the sense of privacy and the openness of the common areas are radicalized. These will form a microstage of sorts that will be partly an extension of the city and partly an extended living room of the occupants, and where, during the course of one summer, lectures, discussions, and workshops are to take place, along with parties and concerts.

The maze replaces the wall "The door," Georges Perec writes, "breaks space in two, splits it […] On one side, me and my place, the private, the domestic […] on the other side, other people, the world, the public, politics. You can't simply let yourself slide from one into the other […] You have to have the password, have to cross the threshold, have to show your credentials, have to communicate, just as the prisoner communicates with the world outside."[120] Could there be a spatial organization that separates the private and the public in a different, graded manner, one that creates maze-like zones between the dwelling units, a jungle of plants that blurs the boundary toward one's neighbor? The maze does not reveal its dimensions; it makes spaces seem bigger. The vegetation extends the private sphere and functions like a filter. The boundary between the intimate and the open is no longer marked by a wall, but rather by a zone that keeps getting denser to the point that one can become lost in it.

What if the street and the bed were not separated by a sequence of doors and walls, but merely a maze?

It takes very little time to climb over a wall or to break open a door. It takes longer to overcome a maze in which one can get lost. At the same time, the social life that one can already observe in the open interstices of Moriyama House can embed

Smooth transitions
Jungle

itself in the maze's niches, winding passages, and coves. Which is not to say that we should instantly do away with all bedroom doors—just that we can, perhaps, reduce to a minimum the number of doors and other isolation or seclusion systems and plan maze-like structures in the spaces that open up, structures that provide protection, a filter, and that at the same time invite rather than exclude. What could something like this look like? Here, too, we can find examples in old Italian villages, where chairs and tables stand on squares no larger than a living room or a kitchen, and where one can find kitchens that open up to courtyards the size of squares.

Crosby Street (Thomas Struth), 1978

Chapter 9

Atmospheres

Housing and what unconsciously affects it

I open the window: we all have an idea of what this sentence means—even of what opening a window feels like. But it makes a difference whether we do this in New York or Paris or Düsseldorf—whether we slightly bend down and push up an American double-hung window or open French doors in a nineteenth-century house, thereby automatically spreading our arms, or whether we clutch at the cold, bare, silvery lever of a Velux window, like a drowning person clinging to a branch, and pull it down. Our body makes different movements and our hand touches different materials.

And it also makes a difference whether what enters the room—through the open window, while a curtain hides the room from view—is street noise or the quiet of a forest. The real nature of a window is determined not just by its form, but also by its materials, the body movements it activates, and the sounds and smells that surround it.

The eye dominates architecture to this day: façades are built to please the eye, windows are created for views and lighting. What is lacking is training that addresses the question of how architecture is experienced directly with the body: how does the wind breeze through this room? What does the wood of the patio smell like when it becomes moist in fog or warm in the sun? What does a brass handle feel like when it is cold, or a plastic switch on a hot day? Being in a particular place and feeling a particular way are related: "Both are linked and, in a way, one: from the way I feel I can tell what kind of space I am in."[121] But what are the factors that determine this feeling? Do I prefer to touch a delicate, filigreed, almost sharp-edged door handle or rather one that is good-naturedly plump, solidly massive? When dealing with a city like Berlin—which doesn't have the piercingly clear air coming from the Atlantic that sometimes flows into the urban canyons of Manhattan—should one build there differently than in New York?

These are all questions that people like to sneeringly dismiss as issues for hypersensitive interior decorators and those with esoteric opinions about materials. Yet the perception of an apartment as too small, too cold, or too claustrophobic often depends on these very questions, as does, ultimately, the architectural quality of a building.

Many houses that are built with cheap materials offer much square footage for little money—and no aura, no atmosphere beyond a dull sense of practicality. No wonder that the anemic blandness of the place is subsequently reworked by the helpless occupants who bring in truckloads of stuff to make it cozier, from pompom lamps and tassels and curtains to cozy sofas and triangular designer jokes, in order to create the atmosphere that the pragmatic residential box is lacking.

It would be a mistake—and futile—to draw up a catalogue of "good" and "bad" atmospheres; individual preferences are too diverse and the historical biases of the perception of architecture too different for anyone to claim with anthropological certainty that this bright glasshouse is too cold and uncomfortable "for human beings" and that spherical house too claustrophobic; one person loves to sleep outdoors in the desert or on a roof terrace and can at most tolerate four glass walls around him, while another person feels lost in the same environment.

Even the perception of a fire in the fireplace depends on individual and historical factors. For a long time the assumption prevailed that smoke was healthy. In his book *At Home*,[122] Bill Bryson recounts that as late as 1577, an author by the name of William Harrison explained that on the days when open fires were burning in the halls of British castles people never had headaches. And while gathering by the fire was long considered an "archaic" moment of community, architects and engineers such as Werner Sobek reject such allegedly anthropologically rooted rituals as ecologically untenable sentimentalism: where one person finds comfort in the glow of a fire, another just sees gratuitous CO_2 emissions that spoil his energy footprint. In the early twentieth century, opulent buildings from the nineteenth century were considered to be the epitome of gaudiness even among conservative architects: Paul Schultze-Naumburg, for instance, complained in 1917 that the residential neighborhoods built in Germany between 1870 and 1914 "are among the most misguided and ugliest that has ever been witnessed in the field of architecture,"[123] while today they are seen as the gold standard of middle-class urban living and fetch the highest prices ever. For this reason alone the study of atmospheres in architecture cannot reveal any supra-individual truths.

Dwelling needs are not static: there are days when one would like to be surrounded by light, steel, and glass and other days when one would rather live in a cave. For both needs, openness and seclusion, a form must be found that avoids claustrophobia on the one hand and a feeling of being exposed on the other. For the construction of residential buildings this would require that one allow potentially multiple atmospheres within a building and not design it as an atmospherically well-defined object, but rather as a flexible stage that can adapt to different moods. Among the simplest means to achieve this are curtains or sliding walls, which allow one to regulate the incidence of light.

Crosby Street (Thomas Struth), 1978
Wilhelm-Tell-Strasse, Düsseldorf (Thomas Struth), 1979

The photographer Thomas Struth has photographed cities for decades, and formally, the scenes often show something very similar: empty streets, parked cars, a city still empty at a seemingly disengaged moment of anticipation. When comparing these images, it becomes obvious that there is a big difference between sinking into the velour seats of a Cadillac while riding through the brick canyons of New York and driving in a metallically roaring Renault 16 through a West German side street with its blackened plaster façades, where the dirt the wind has carried from the Ruhr covers the soot left by the wartime night bombing of the region—a very different kind of dirt than the dark dirt in Italy and a different darkness from that of the heavy brick buildings of Manhattan. The different details of things change perception. When the rule still applied in France that all cars should be equipped with yellow headlights, the French nights in Paris seemed darker, warmer, and more mysterious to the foreign eye: the light of the city was subdued. In 1993, a new EU norm required that all new cars be equipped with white headlights, and ever since the light in French cities has become colder; only once in a while, when an old Renault drives through a side street, does the old atmosphere briefly return. And the gray-blue dilapidated façades and dull colors of East Berlin were also perceived through the filter of a smell: even with your eyes closed, you knew you were in East Berlin—the bluish smell of thousands of two-stroke engines gave it away.

Paradox atmospheres

Maybe it is impossible to separate "good" from "bad" atmospheres, but one can distinguish spaces with a clear atmosphere—like the clinical, almost medically sterile, all-over steel-white buildings of Richard Meier—from spaces with paradox atmospheres, which characterize, for instance, some of the residences of Frank Lloyd Wright, such as Fallingwater, a residence he designed for Edgar Kaufmann, a Pittsburgh businessman and owner of a department store. Built between 1935 and 1937 on a small waterfall in the Allegheny Mountains about 50 miles southeast of Pittsburgh, its interiors are particularly interesting, with walls shaped like rocks and large flagstone rather than tile flooring, including a few boulders that protrude through the floor into the room. The interior with its narrow, slit-like windows on the one hand feels like a cave, an extremely intimate space, and on the other as if one were outside on a smoothed rocky plateau. In perception the space thus shifts between extreme interiority and exteriority. Although the client wanted to be able to see the waterfall from the house, the architect famously decided to build the house with its cantilevered balconies on top of the waterfall, so that it was not visible, its rushing and splashing, however, all the more present acoustically. In this way Fallingwater became architecture that collapses distance, a house that pushes back the dominance of the visual.

Various shades of brightness and darkness also play a role in the perception of the building. In 1933, just before construction on

Fallingwater began, the Japanese novelist Jun'ichiro Tanizaki wrote an essay titled "In Praise of Shadows," in which he developed an aesthetic that asks how particular atmospheres are evoked, for

Ackerberg House, Malibu
(Richard Meier)
Fallingwater, Mill Run
(Frank Lloyd Wright)

instance, in architecture. To Tanizaki, the appeal of everyday Japanese objects depended above all on light: the bright, electric European light, he claimed, robs ceramic dishes and the dark bowls with black lacquer of their magic, causing them to appear straightforward and dull in a vulgar way devoid of all mystery. Only twilight brings out the quality of its surfaces, a shimmering and flickering, an indefiniteness, like a veiling, a constant transformation, a promise of new surprises and unsuspected effects. In this case it is the twilight that is orchestrated by means of the translucent paper walls and dark wood panels of Japanese houses, which evokes a certain atmosphere where contours and boundaries dissolve and maintain a tense equilibrium of visibility and invisibility—just like an ambiguous image that keeps producing new effects. And because the twilight confounds the eye, the other senses are sharpened: the object is touched, smelled, the

sounds of the tea being poured into the cup and of the wind chimes are perceived more intensely. In this way architecture immersed in semidarkness sharpens the senses of its occupants.

All this is part of the architectural form: the drawing of its contours is but one part of it. The others are wind, light, haptics, narrowness, capaciousness, sounds and smells of the surroundings. In New York, these are the Atlantic air, the howling of sirens and the squealing of seagulls, warmth rising from underground, the summer heat that, more than elsewhere, stagnates in the urban canyons and is stored in the stone façades. In Paris, they are the muted light from the cafés, the hot and sticky smell of the métro in which the heated rubber of the wheels blends with a slight mustiness, the warm muffled sound of doors closing. Any house that is built in such an environment will, consciously or unconsciously, inscribe itself into those atmospheres.

The control of perception in commercial space

One reason why architects need to start dealing with the subject of atmospheres is that the question of how to control human behavior by means of atmospheres is by now also an object of highly specialized research that mainly pursues very real economic goals. "The combination of citrus scent and cleanliness has already etched itself deeply into the human brain," a study of the magazine *Ökotest* explains. "Students who were exposed to the fragrance of a lemon-scented cleaner kept their table cleaner during mealtime than a non-exposed control group did."[124]

German supermarket chains such as Edeka are testing, together with the Hamburg-based Audio Consulting Group and the Department of Psychology of the University of Mannheim, the effect that classical music has on buying behavior in the wine aisle. Synthetic fragrances are used to bolster the desired atmosphere. "Thus jets installed in the wine section by the company Air Creative emit a combination of whiffs of cinnamon and cardamom to put customers into a buying mood. In the drinks section, on the other hand, a citrus fragrance is used to suggest freshness to the consumers,"[125] while red light above the meat counter serves to make steaks and chops appear fresh.

Gate of Janus, Rome

Chapter 10

Change the Laws!

For a New Building Policy

Veduta dell'Arco di Giano

Housing, bureaucracy, capitalism

Unimaginative architects like to point out that cities reflect societal processes: that every society gets the houses, squares, and cities it deserves. This self-imposed depressive action inhibition of architecture suits all those who, for economic reasons, are not interested in transforming building, such as the manufacturers of solid houses, roofing shingles, PVC windows, and insulating plaster. But the very reason why houses and squares look so desperate is that those readily identifiable players earn a lot of money with increasing standardization, which they like to pass off as inevitable, and therefore understandably have no interest in fundamental change—and the fact that politicians make shortsighted decisions, such as selling state-owned properties in city centers to investors.

Yet profitability and urban life do not need to be mutually exclusive, as the example of the Überseequartier in Hamburg shows, namely, that going by alleged economic necessities by no means ensures economic prosperity—in this case it compounded a financial disaster with an urbanist one.

The argument that buildings cannot change a society is usually just an excuse for ineptitude: if architecture were indeed unable to change anything, then its unimaginative appearance wouldn't be so bad. Fortunately, we have come to the end of the depressing phase in the history of architecture, when architects tried to justify their well-tempered unimaginativeness by claiming that the era of grand designs had ended and that utopian architectural projects brought nothing but misery upon cities and the people living in them.

There is new architecture which shows that things do not have to be this way. This new architecture has the quality of a social model—in this sense it is political—that provides new spaces for new experiences, needs, and rituals.

Times are good for architects. There are many more interesting approaches to creating new housing and construction than there have been in a long time. As discussed earlier, many of the great crises of the present are essentially crises of space: the financial crisis, climate change, the desolation of city centers and the social segregation linked to it, even the related issue of access to educational and information resources.

What are the implications of this? No new approach will change the architecture of the cities and suburbs if the political conditions for building do not change. Many see the plight of construction as an inextricable, complex tangle of a variety of factors whose cause lies in the murkiness of regulations and interests. But that is not true. One can clearly pinpoint the framework conditions that afflict the culture of building, that prevent new forms—and what would need to be changed.

Legislation as a design device

To create affordable living space in the city would not even require building state-financed subsidized houses with cheap apartments. As mentioned earlier, just changing political regulations governing construction would do it; such as permitting the eaves height in cities like Berlin, where it is usually not allowed to exceed 72 feet, to be raised to 85 feet—and thus allowing the construction of penthouse apartments under the condition that the owner, in return, commits to renting one floor at 0.6 euro per square foot. This would allow private homeowners to construct attractive penthouse apartments that can be rented at high prices and at the same time create thousands of affordable apartments.

Money for communities
The concept of planning value compensation

Wherever construction takes place, a zoning map or land-use plan is needed, which is really supposed to be drawn up by the communities. But because those communities often do not have the money to hire employees who would look at architectural quality and put juries together to discuss what is considered desirable in buildings, "project-based development plans" of private investors are increasingly waved through. If a community has a field that has not yet been classified as building land and a private investor wants to build thirty homes there, he can draw up a development plan and enter into an urban-planning contract with the community, so that it becomes applicable planning law. Because planning is expensive, communities are happy when the investor provides the plan. Usually, however, the investor has no interest in promoting new forms of housing that are expensive to plan and less profitable. As a result, new housing developments look, in fact, like profit motives congealed into houses.

"There is a commodization of interests in building," says Thomas Kaup, regional chairman of the Association of German Architects in Berlin. "Costs and deadlines are greatly prioritized, so that architectural quality is often barely a subject of discussion anymore."

How could communities afford planners and regain sovereignty over design? When a community makes land available for building, the value of that site goes up, yet the development costs are to be borne by the public authorities. The profit the landowner makes as a result of the community's actions could be returned to the public purse as planning value compensation and spent on planners, as outlined by a 1998 German legislative proposal. If there is no planning value compensation, then the communities do not take in any funds and are forced to swallow "project-based development plans" or to just go by the existing building stock. Hence the same forms are favored over and over again and nothing really new will be built.

Changing building regulations
Separation principle and isolation mania

The laws and regulations covering construction still reflect, to a far too large extent, 1950s urban-planning ideology. Maximum density regulations can be historically understood as an attempt to prevent the unhygienic living conditions that used to exist in the courtyard and damp basement apartments of the late nineteenth century. But today, high-density development does not automatically have to be stuffy, dark, and damp, especially since it is used differently. Yet building it is made very difficult. The allowed development density is a problem—the compact European city loved by millions of tourists could no longer be built under these conditions. Even the 1987 International Building Exhibition in Berlin, which was still financed with public housing funds, already suffered badly from applicable building regulations: no commercial use in the courtyards, no stores at each corner—this lack of mixed use still hurts the buildings today.

Other well-intentioned regulations should also be reviewed: the Energy Saving Ordinance may be useful in principle when it comes to building cost-effectively and using space effectively, but it should be allowed to forgo extreme thermal insulation in some cases. Not in every room do temperature levels have to meet the exorbitant comfort ideals of a society that demands a cozy 78 degrees or higher, even when it is zero degrees out in the hallway; not every attic needs to be reachable by elevator. If people demand the highest standards in everything, they should not complain when construction becomes more and more expensive. In this respect the German building code would need to be probed for its tendency toward excesses of comfort.

Joint building ventures and adaptive reuse
Self-empowerment of residents and architects

The greatest innovations in residential architecture are currently driven by a phenomenon called "joint building ventures," a self-help movement of sorts: people who want to build a home for themselves join forces and build something they cannot find in the marketplace—architecture that allows them to live the way they envisage as part of a larger group and that often differs greatly from the profitable stacking of mid-size apartments in purely functional buildings. Architects do not wait like a depressed private detective for a client to show up and finally give them a job: they commission themselves, design a residential building, and then look for people who would like to live exactly that way. The prototype for a new "colony" in Berlin is just one example of this self-empowerment of a generation of younger architects and urban activists.

Communities could promote this model: they could put out to tender building sites where publicly funded architects would coordinate multiple joint building ventures as project director.

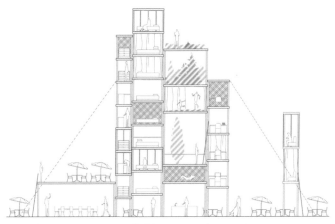

Berlin colony, 2016 (Experimentalkollektiv Bauen with June 14)

Conversions

In Germany, the new building rate is one percent. Much more consideration should be given to the adaptive reuse of state-owned building stock: can a municipal or federal building be turned into a residential building? Can a parking garage be converted into student housing with a gigantic roof terrace? State housing promotion could organize architectural design competitions for such projects as well.

Ultimately, the state is still involved in deciding what a new development area will look like—for instance, whether private investors are obligated to build a particular percentage of social housing when they want to buy building land, or whether planning value compensation is introduced. Instead of being statist patronizing, such regulations would simply be an instrument to keep the city alive as a social construction. The fact that in most major cities in Europe and North America you can leave a Porsche out on the street without fear that it will immediately be stolen or that you will have a gun to your head at the next stoplight, is also due to a social market economy that recognized worry-free housing, among other things, as a cornerstone of social stability.

Government building policies are traditionally assailed with the argument that in a free society everyone should be allowed to build the way they want. That they would be able to do so as soon as the state pulls back is one of the greatest fallacies of liberalism. When the state forgoes building codes and development plans, it is not the sovereign citizen who comes into his own; rather, the building industry, along with the lobbies of the turn-key ready, will dictate the way people dwell. The housing models that will end up dominating are the ones that are most profitable.

We must ask ourselves what it is we give up when the business of housing building is left predominantly to the private sector, to investors whose primary interests do not include experimental or social architecture. Public housing associations in Europe struggle with a different structural problem. Now that funding for social housing has been cut and authorities prefer to distribute the funds previously used for housing in the form of personal rent subsidies, thereby supporting people and, by consequence, privately funded housing construction, the housing associations have reduced to a bare minimum the number of employees who dealt with new construction. Because housing has become a campaign issue, they are once again called upon to ensure expeditious construction of thousands of apartments; by 2030, thirteen thousand apartments annually are to be produced out of thin air in Berlin alone. The housing associations, however, have barely any planners left, so this job is largely assigned to general contractors whose project directors try above all to stay on time and budget. And because all those involved are under huge pressure to meet the target, they tend toward tried and tested solutions, meaning the usual energy-optimized, dull building blocks with protruding steel balconies they have already built a thousand times. This leaves little room for experiments, adventures, innovative ideas that passionate politicians, urban planners, and architects could push through—especially since the funds for international building exhibitions are also being cut, as they recently have been in Berlin. In this way we run the risk that some kind of housing is constructed, but not the kind that responds to a changed society.

Of course, the state does spend hundreds of millions on housing. In Germany, social housing is to be revived and for this purpose the individual *Bundesländer* are to receive 518 million euros annually in funding through 2019. Except that what is—and what will be—built there and elsewhere is, in the vast majority of cases, more of the same: practical, desolate, thick, elongated, fully insulated, aesthetically dismal residential shelves that are cheap to build and thus ideal for the building industry. Hundreds of millions of euros are dumped into the wrong buildings, which are built around lifestyles and residents that do not even exist. In order to arrive at fundamentally different architecture it is not only necessary to change laws and ordinances, such as dogmatic noise control regulations, but also to provide funds for research into and promotion of new forms of housing.

Every good house proves that architecture can change society and lifestyles: any house in which the isolation of the occupants is abolished; in which people have breakfast on a roof terrace or in a conservatory rather than in a dark kitchen; in which the children can run from the kitchen into a huge communal, jungle-like garden; in which neighbors can meet, if they feel like it, in common spaces; any house that does away with the separation between work and living areas and combines both in a new kind of dwelling landscape that also fosters a new form of microeconomy and local production; any house that proves that there are other conceivable ways of dwelling and lifestyles beyond the model of a "home for singles or nuclear families"—such as homes for six octogenarians who do not want to move to a retirement home, or homes for three single parents with five children and a gay couple.

Any house where one's monthly rent or mortgage payment is lower, because it has been planned and built more intelligently, and one can thus live more relaxed and freer, changes society.

What is still missing is energetic public encouragement of such architecture. Why do the major cities not organize an international architecture competition for the design of new municipal housing which responds to the demographic changes as well as to the changes in lifestyles and social rituals—and then also actually build a couple of those houses as "Case Study Houses"? If such houses were a success, it would also convince private residential developers to try out new models.

The issue of new standardization in construction with plain but not bleakly profit-oriented forms should also be made a research area of habitology. Only by adopting new strategies can one escape the pressure of standardization exerted by the building industry, which makes billions on dismal apartment blocks and cheap and depressing, pseudo-individual houses.

The biggest problem of architectural thought, however, is language, because the design is preceded by thinking in concepts, because language influences and shapes the production of forms. Could a house be a sponge? Is housing without walls and doors conceivable? A high-rise without floors? A house like a forest? A single-family residence where twenty people can live as a family? All these questions need to be asked.

The Room of Janus

If we think further from where Expo 67 and Moshe Safdie's clustered housing project left off, it would be possible to create architecture in which people live very differently: because it can be assembled from prefab elements, it is less expensive to build and the pressure to earn money diminishes—provided the builders pass on the savings to the occupants, which requires political framework conditions. People could then work less and relax and simply enjoy their homes more. First models exist. Because they offer what people have been looking for in the countryside—gardens, spaces to rest and relax, the village idyll—the stress of commuting to work every day is eliminated. What these designs hint at most of all is a different model of society. The spatial organization creates zones that make it easier to invite passersby or a friend who happens to drop by, easier to allow children to play at the neighbors' and with friends, easier to respond to situations that would be considered a problem in the inflexible houses that are built around the nuclear family.

The public and the private are defined differently—based on a wide intermediate zone. This applies to the space, but also to the notion of what a family, a community is.

The oversize kitchen doubling as a semipublic place stands for this new type that limits the private, the retreat area to a small core cell. This limitation does not have to be an imposition, as new Japanese architecture shows. If it works, the more intimate rooms become even more secure and protective, more cave- or nest-like as a result of their concentration. One could call it a radicalization of housing: the spaces intended for retreat and those intended for encounter and communication are organized more decisively, with the former becoming more isolated and the latter more inviting.

The opposite of common conceptions of houses, squares, and streets would be a public living room, an inversion of space of the kind found in old Italian towns where tables are suddenly moved to the middle of the street, or between the residential cubes and in the collective kitchens of new Japanese architecture.

Habitat 67, Montreal (Moshe Safdie)

Roman mythology has created an image for such inside-outside or internal-external inversions: that of the two-faced god Janus, who gave the nymph Cardea power over thresholds, door hinges, and door handles. It is not a coincidence that the name of the god for whom front and rear and inside and outside do not exist and who always looks both forward and backward, inside and outside belongs to the same word family as *ianua*, the term for door, and *ianus*, the open passage, that is, for places where identity and other, publicness and property do not need to be conceived of as irreconcilable opposites.

Notes

Preface

1   Michael Kimmelman, "Trading Parking Lots for Affordable Housing,"
    in *The New York Times*, September 14, 2014, Art & Design section.
2   Andrea Elliot, "Girl in the Shadows: Dasani's Homeless Life,"
    in *The New York Times*, December 9, 2013.
3   Klaus Drömer et al., *Housing for everyone. Affordable living*
    (Berlin 2014), p.13.
4   Tobias Just, "Eine Milliarde neue Wohnungen," in
    Frankfurter Allgemeine Zeitung, January 22, 2010. For further details,
    see also Tobias Just, *Demographie und Immobilien* (Munich 2009).
5   Data on population structure compiled in a survey by GfK, Nuremberg, 2011.
6   Hans Kollhoff, "Gib mir Simse: Was ist zeitgemäßes Bauen,"
    in *Frankfurter Allgemeine Zeitung*, May 12, 2011, no. 110, p. 30.
7   Gert Selle, *Die eigenen vier Wände. Zur verborgenen Geschichte des Wohnens*
    (Frankfurt am Main 1996), p. 11.
8   Ibid., p. 17.
9   Hartmut Häußermann and Walter Siebel, *Soziologie des Wohnens*
    (Weinheim/Munich 1996), pp. 11–12.
10 Study by the Empirica research institute for the Berlin head office of LBS,
    Germany's state building and loan association, 2005; http://empirica-institut.
    de/kufa/empi123rb.pdf [accessed July 13, 2015].
11 Susanne Schindler, lecture at the symposium "Architecture and Democracy,"
    Princeton, February 21, 2014.
12 Carmela Ferraro: "Small but perfectly formed," in *Financial Times*,
    February 21, 2009.
13 On the small house movement, see also Sarah Susanka,
    Kira Obolensky: *The Not So Big House: A Blueprint for the Way We Really
    Live* (Newtown, CT 2008); and Eckhard Tollkühn: *Auf kleinstem Raum*,
    in *Süddeutsche Zeitung,* August 12, 2011.
14 Dr. Wolfgang Feist: *Graue Energie und Passivhaus – Welche Bedeutung hat
    der Energieaufwand für die Herstellung?* Passivhaus-Institut; http://www.
    passivhaustagung.de/Passivhaus_D/Graue_Energie_und_Passivhaus_2007.htm
    [accessed June 1, 2015].
15 Schindler (see note 10).
16 See, among others, John Gallagher: "Housing in Detroit," in *Detroit Free Press*,
    2010; Louis Aguilar, "Ilitches set affordable housing goal in epic plans," in
    The Detroit News, March 26, 2015; Logan Anjaneyulu, *Building Rehabilita-
    tion: A Promising Tool for Urban Revitalization in Detroit, Michigan* (Michigan
    State University, Construction Management Program, 2003); Larry R. Ford,
    America's New Downtowns: Revitalization or Reinvention (Baltimore 2003).
17 Robert Sharoff, "National Perspectives: Waves of Renovations Helping
    Downtown Detroit," in *The New York Times*, January 30, 2005.
18 Such as Marcos L. Rosa et al., *Handmade Urbanism – From Community
    Initiatives to Participatory Models* (Berlin 2013).

Chapter 1-10

1   Nicola Kuhn, "Andy Warhol legt im Museumshafen an," in *Tagesspiegel*,
     June 18, 2008.

2   In European city centers, too, designed private gardens replace rampant
     community gardens: the same real estate developer that is bestowing the
     Kronprinzengärten on the center of Berlin, Bauwert Investment Group, put up
     eleven seven-story buildings with 70 rental apartments and 144 condos for just
     under 100 million euros on the grounds of the former Württemberg community
     garden in the western part of the city; buildings will cover 40 percent of the
     150,000-square-foot area and representative designed gardens the rest.
     The average price per square foot for the ensemble conceived by the Berlin-
     based architecture office of Arno Bonanni and Patzschke & Partners was 380
     euros. The community garden life was pushed out of the city—and with it a
     social group that no longer could afford the neighborhood anyhow. The entity
     selling the property was not interested in a solution combining high-priced
     development with preservation of the community garden and a social mix, and
     this seller was not just some individual, but rather the city: Bauwert had bought
     the former community garden area in the Wilmersdorf area of Berlin from the
     Berliner Liegenschaftsfonds.

3   The entry with the research data this chapter refers to was deleted
     after the publication of the author's article "Architekten auf die Barrikaden,"
     in *Frankfurter Allgemeine Zeitung*, November 26, 2011.

4   Extensive information regarding the Haus Flair 113 was taken from the
     excellent article "Deutsches Haus" by Harald Willenbrock, in *Brand eins*
     (October 10, 2013): 86–92, here p. 88.

5   Ibid.

6   Ibid., p. 89.

7   Ibid., p. 92.

8   Ibid., p. 90.

9   Ibid., p. 89.

10   Ibid., p. 92.

11   Ibid.

12   Ibid.

13   Ibid., p. 90.

14   Ibid., p. 92.

15   Roger-Henri Guerrand, "Private Spaces," in Philippe Ariès and George Duby
     (eds.), *A History of Private Life* (Cambridge, MA 1990), vol. 4, pp. 331–417,
     here p. 401.

16   Ralph Martin, "Vergesst die Großstadt," in *Frankfurter Allgemeine
     Sonntagszeitung*, January 27, 2013.

17   Lauri Apple, "Brooklynites Blessing the Hudson Valley with Hipness,"
     in *The New York Times* online, June 8, 2011.

18   Richard Sennett, *The Fall of Public Man* (New York 1977).

19   http://osthessen-news.de/A/1148528/huenfeld-rote-daecher-oder-regenerativ-
     solarenergie-neue-gestaltungsverordnung.html [accessed June 1, 2015].

20 For the solar tile, see http://www.panotron.com/solarsystem.htm?idp=85 [accessed June 1, 2015].

21 Claude Parent in conversation with the author, June 2010.

22 Ibid.

23 See also Wolfram Hoepfner, "Die Epoche der Griechen," in Hoepfner (ed.), *Geschichte des Wohnens*, vol. 1, *5000 v. Chr. – 500 n. Chr.* (Stuttgart 1999), here p. 148

24 Chloé Parent, "Privilégiée," in Claude Parent, *L'oeuvre construite, l'oeuvre graphique, présentée à la cité de l'architecture & du patrimoine du 20 janvier au 2 mai 2010*, pp. 17–18.

25 http://de.lifestyle.yahoo.com/die-10-meist-verkauften-ikea-produkte.html [accessed June 1, 2015].

26 Hoepfner, "Die Epoche der Griechen" (see note 23), p. 138.

27 Helen Murray, *Friends Forever*, Lego DK Readers (2012), p. 8

28 Ibid., p. 10.

29 Ibid.

30 Adelheid von Saldern, "Wohnen im Spannungsfeld von Gegebenheiten und Aneignungen," in *Geschichte des Wohnens*, ed. Jürgen Reulecke (Stuttgart 1997), vol. 3, p. 254.

31 Pascal Dibie, *Wie man sich bettet. Die Kulturgeschichte des Schlafzimmers* (Stuttgart 1989), p. 69 (original French ed.: *Ethnologie de la chambre à coucher* [Paris 2000]).

32 Orest Ranum, "Refugien der Intimität," in Philippe Ariès, *Geschichte des privaten Lebens*, vol. 3, pp. 216–69, here p. 221 (Engl. ed., *History of Private Life*, vol. 3 [Cambridge, MA 1993]).

33 Hartmut Häußermann and Walter Siebel, *Soziologie des Wohnens* (Weinheim/Munich 1996), p. 36.

34 Karlheinz Graudenz and Erica Pappritz, *Etikette neu* (Munich 1971), p. 48

35 Ernst Bloch, *Das Prinzip Hoffnung*, in Bloch, *Gesamtausgabe*, vol. 5 (Frankfurt am Main 1985), p. 859 (Engl. ed., *The Principle of Hope* [Cambridge, MA 1986]).

36 Sou Fujimoto, *Primitive Future*, Contemporary Architect's Concept Series no. 1 (Tokyo 2008).

37 http://www.architekten-schindhelm-moser.de/pavillon-munchen/ [accessed June 1, 2015].

38 www.schueco.com/web/asset/de/.../p3757-sch_co_thermoslide_1.pdf [accessed June 1, 2015].

39 Originally available online at http://profloeffler.files.wordpress.com/2012/10/ando.pdf.

40 www.archplus.net/home/archiv/artikel/46,302,1,0.html [accessed June 1, 2015].

41 Walter Benjamin, *The Arcades Project* (Cambridge, MA 1999), p. 220.

42 See also Niklas Maak, "Jenseits von Entenhausen. Wie der Disney-Konzern einen Zustand vorindustrieller Unschuld vortäuscht," in *Süddeutsche Zeitung*, January 16, 1999.

43 Julia Voss, "Bild der Frau," in *Frankfurter Allgemeine Zeitung*, September 6, 2008, p. 42.

44 Claudia Liedtke, "Rom und Ostia," in Hoepfner, *Geschichte des Wohnens* (see note 23), pp. 685–735, here p. 685.

45 See also Thomas Niperdey, *Deutsche Geschichte 1800-1866. Bürgerwelt und starker Staat* (Munich 1983); and Jürgen Reulecke, "Die Mobilisierung der Kräfte und Kapitale: Der Wandel der Lebensverhältnisse im Gefolge von Industrialisierung und Verstädterung," in Hoepfner (ed.), *Geschichte des Wohnens*, vol. 3 (Stuttgart 1997), pp. 17ff.

46 Jürgen Habermas, *The Structural Transformation of the Public Sphere: An Inquiry into a Category of Bourgeois Society* (Cambridge 1989), p. 45.

47 See also Wolfram Hoepfner. "Die Epoche der Griechen," in Gerhard Zimmer, "Handwerkliche Arbeit im Umfeld des Wohnens," in Wolfram Hoepfner (ed.), *Geschichte des Wohnens*, vol. 1, *5000 v. Chr. – 500 n. Chr* (Stuttgart 1999), pp. 123–609, here p. 144.

48 Emile Cheysson, Report on the workers' settlement Passy-Auteuil, *Economiste francais*, August 27, 1881, quoted by Roger-Henri Guerrand, "Private Spaces" (see note 15), p. 424.

49 Quoted by Hartmut Häußermann and Walter Siebel, *Soziologie des Wohnens* (Weinheim/Munich 1996), p. 131.

50 On Fourier, see, among others, François Dagognet, *Trois philosophes revisitées: Saint-Simon, Proudhon, Fourier* (Hildesheim, Zurich, and New York 1997); and Franziska Bollerey's seminal work *Architekturkonzeptionen der utopischen Sozialisten: alternative Planung und Architektur für den gesellschaftlichen Prozess* (Munich and Berlin 1977/1991).

51 See Guerrand, "Private Spaces" (see note 15), p. 404.

52 Charles Fourier, *The New Amorous World*, in ibid., pp. 404–05.

53 Charles Fourier, *False Industry*, in ibid., pp. 404–05.

54 On Considerant, see especially Jonathan Beecher, *Victor Considerant and the Rise and Fall of French Romantic Socialism* (Berkeley, Los Angeles, and London 2001).

55 All homes had access to a glass-covered passage, a biosphere of sorts that was to provide shade in the summer and to be heated in the winter. This gallery was to be "the channel through which life circulates through the great phalansterian body." "Man is not made to live in caves. He is not a burrowing animal. [...] Is it easier to house 1,800 in the middle of the ocean, 1,800 leagues from the nearest shore, than to house 1,800 peasants in a harmonious building in the middle of Champagne or Beauce?"

56 Gabriele Stauner-Linder, *Die Société du Familistere de Guise des j.-B. A. Godin* (Frankfurt am Main 1984), p. 38.

57 Franziska Bollerey, *Architekturkonzeptionen der utopischen Sozialisten: alternative Planung und Architektur für den gesellschaftlichen Prozess* (Munich and Berlin 1977/1991), p. 140.

58 See also Guerrand, "Private Spaces" (see note 15), p. 409.

59 Jules Moureau, Des Associations coopératives, 1866; discussed in depth by Guerrand, "Private Spaces" (see note 15), p. 411.

60 Ibid., p. 412.

61 Ibid.

62 On this in depth, see Clemens Zimmermann, "Wohnen als sozialpolitische Herausforderung," in Wolfram Hoepfner (ed.), *Geschichte des Wohnens*, vol. 3 (Stuttgart 1997), p. 542.

63 Jules Verne, *The Begum's Millions* (Middletown, CT 2014), pp. 54–55.

64 Ibid., pp. 130–31.

65 Dietrich Neumann points out that these ideals still informed the garden city ideals of Tony Garnier and the architectural ideals of Le Corbusier: Dietrich Neumann, entry on Jules Verne, in Winfried Nerdinger (ed.), *Architektur wie sie im Buche steht. Fiktive Bauten und Städte in der Literatur* (Munich 2006), p. 298.

66 Zimmermann, "Wohnen als sozialpolitische Herausforderung" (see note 62), p. 604.

67 See Guerrand, "Private Spaces" (see note 15), p. 419.

68 Ibid., p. 420.

69 Ibid.

70 German Federal Statistical Office, press release no. 233, July 11, 2013.

71 Yoshiharu Tsukamoto, "Fourth-Generation Houses and Void Metabolism," from *Tokyo Metabolizing*, in "Tokyo, die Stadt bewohnen," *Arch+* 208 (August 2012): "Eventually things reached the point where it seemed unnatural for anyone outside the family to be in the house, and the space became a purely domestic domain. The lack of invited guests led to closed houses and, coupled with the spread of air-conditioning, exterior spaces around the houses, such as the eaves and the garden, decreased significantly. Due to an increase in subdivision and a more restrictive building-coverage code, the exterior walls of the structures began to push at the limits of the lot, and house construction became little more than a by-product of these gaps. From these characteristics, one detects a trend toward overall intolerance in residential spaces. Isn't there a way of curtailing this interactive spiral of intolerance and creating tolerant spaces that are more conducive to living through the medium of housing?

    In an attempt to achieve this, we have established three conditions that are necessary for fourth-generation houses: 1) bringing people from outside the family back inside the house; 2) increasing the opportunities to dwell outside the house; 3) redefining the gaps. Fortunately, with the diffusion of the cell phone, technologies of granulation, and the pressure of capitalism have been released from the house. In other words, fourth-generation houses have been liberated from this program of individuation and granulation. This makes it even more likely that we may be able to redirect the focus of residential architecture toward community and collectivity. In other words, by determining the behavior of each individual structure through the resonance that occurs between intermediate units and the city as a limited whole, and by establishing a fourth generation of houses in respect to the lineage of the previous three generations of detached houses that are combined within it, we find the potential to liberate houses from the programs of granulation and intolerance that came with the agenda of ownership in the 20th century and create tolerant spaces where people can live a more vital life."

72 On this, see also Dieter Hoffmann-Axthelm, "Die Wohnungsfrage," in Hoffmann-Axthelm, *Die dritte Stadt* (Frankfurt 1993), pp. 149–52.

73 Cf. Jens Arne Dickmann, "Der Fall Pompeji," in Zimmer, "Handwerkliche Arbeit im Umfeld des Wohnens" (see note 47), pp. 609–79, here p. 660.

74 For the comparison of the Kollektivhuset to a hotel, see also Steinfeld in Staffan Lamm, Thomas Steinfeld, *Das Kollektivhaus. Utopie und Wirklichkeit eines Wohnexperiments* (Frankfurt 2006), pp. 57–58.

236

75 Lamm in ibid., p. 16.
76 Steinfeld in ibid., p. 55.
77 Ibid., p. 67.
78 Cooperative Models, in Klaus Dömer, Hans Drexler, and Joachim Schultz-Granberg (eds.), *Affordable Living. Housing for Everyone*. (Berlin 2014), p. 55.
79 Adelheid von Saldern, "Wohnen im Spannungsfeld von Gegebenheiten und Aneignungen," in Wolfram Hoepfner (ed.), *Geschichte des Wohnens* (Stuttgart 1997), vol. 3, p. 233.
80 Adalbert Stifter, *Indian Summer*, trans. Wendell Fyreb (Bern 2006), p. 8.
81 Zimmer, "Handwerkliche Arbeit im Umfeld des Wohnens" (see note 47), pp. 561–76, here p. 561.
82 Ibid.
83 Arno Kose, Alter Orient und Ägypten, in Zimmer, "Handwerkliche Arbeit im Umfeld des Wohnens" (see note 47), pp. 13–85, here pp. 67–68.
84 For this, see Wolfram Hoepfner, "Die Epoche der Griechen," in Gerhard Zimmer, "Handwerkliche Arbeit im Umfeld des Wohnens," in *Geschichte des Wohnens*, vol. 1, pp. 123–609, here p. 131.
85 Ibid.
86 Ibid., p. 140.
87 Ibid., p. 141.
88 Ibid., p. 144.
89 Ibid.
90 Raymond Geuss, *Public Goods, Private Goods* (Princeton 2001), pp. 106–07.
91 Ibid., p. 105.
92 Sir Thomas More, *Utopia*, trans. Robert M. Adams (New York 1975), p. 38.
93 Jean Marie Goulemot, Literary Practices: Publicizing the Private, in Philippe Ariès and Georges Duby (eds.), *A History of Private Life* (Cambridge, MA 1989), vol. 3, pp. 363–95, here p. 379.
94 Ibid., pp. 379–80.
95 Roland Barthes, *How to Live Together* (New York 2013), p. 54.
96 Raymond Geuss, *Public Goods, Private Goods*, p. 88.
97 Ibid., p. 35.
98 Ibid., p. 40.
99 Madeleine Foisil, "The Literature of Intimacy," in Ariès and Duby (eds.), *History of Private Life* (see note 93), vol. 3, p. 339.
100 Ibid., pp. 339–41.
101 Jacques Derrida, *Adieu to Emanuel Levinas* (Stanford 1999), p. 51.
102 For an in-depth discussion, see Mark W. Westmoreland, in Westmoreland, "Interruptions: Derrida and Hospitality," *Kritiken*, vol. II, no. 1 (June 2008): 1–10, here p. 2.
103 Derrida, *Adieu* (see note 101), p. 50.
104 Jacques Derrida, "The Future of the Profession and the University without Condition," in *Jacques Derrida and the Humanities: A Critical Reader*, ed. Tom Cohen (Cambridge 2002), p. 26.
105 For this, see also Constant Nieuwenhuys, *New Babylon. A Nomadic City*, exh. cat. (The Hague 1974); and in depth, Mark Wigley (ed.), *Constant's New Babylon. The Hyper-Architecture of Desire* (Rotterdam 1998).
106 Nicolas Schöffer, *La ville cybernétique* (Paris 1969).
107 Ibid., p. 86.a

108 "When you talk to people who live in Celebration, you'll hear a lot about front-porch friendliness they found missing in suburbia," in "Just ask a neighbor," promotion brochure of Celebration Realty Inc. (Orlando 1998), p. 2.

109 FBI statistics for the year 2012; see http://www.fbi.gov/about-us/cjis/ucr/crime-in-the-u.s/2012/crime-in-the-u.s.-2012/violent-crime/murder/murder-main [accessed June 1, 2015].

110 http://articles.orlandosentinel.com/2013-01-23/news/os-celebration-hatchet-murder-trial-20130123_1_coin-collection-murder-investigation-first-murder [accessed June 1, 2015].

111 See also Marc Angélil and Rainer Hehl, *Building Brazil* (Zurich and Berlin 2012), pp. 3ff.

112 Justin McGuirk, in *Beyond Torre David* (Berlin 2013), p. 32.

113 United Nations Human Settlements Program. The Challenge of Slums: Global Report on Human Settlements (Nairobi 2003).

114 Report of the Merco Press Agency dated October 7, 2011.

115 Rainer Hehl, in Marc Angélil and Rainer Hehl, *Building Brazil*, p. 6.

116 See also Marcos L. Rosa and Ute E. Weiland, *Handmade Urbanism* (Berlin 2013), p. 68.

117 See also Hanno Rauterberg, *Wir sind die Stadt!* (Frankfurt am Main 2013).

118 The author created a first sketch for such a building during a conversation with Hans-Ulrich Obrist and curators of the Museum of Modern Art in New York on January 16, 2013. Subsequently the project was supervised by Pedro Gadanho of MoMA's department of architecture and the author. The building contract was awarded to the Argentinian firm A77, while Jenny Schlenzka was responsible for the programming. The Colony was in operation from June until early September 2013; see also www.momaps1.org/expo1/module/colony [accessed June 1, 2015].

119 Design by Niklas Maak with June 14 Meyer-Grohbrügge & Chermayeff.

120 Georges Perec, *Species of Spaces and Other Pieces* (London and New York 1999), p. 37.

121 Gernot Böhme, *Architektur und Atmospäre* (Munich 2006), p. 122.

122 Bill Bryson, *At Home. A Short Story of Private Life* (London 2013), pp. 72–73.

123 Paul Schultze-Naumburg, *Der Bau des Wohnhauses* (Munich 1917), preface, n.p.

124 http://www.oekotest.de/cgi/index.cgi?artnr=93781&bernr=09 [accessed June 1, 2015].

125 Ibid.

Picture Credits

The Publisher has made every effort to trace all copyright owners. Individuals and institutions who may not have been contacted but claim rights to the illustrations used are asked to contact the Publisher.

p. 9: © photo Localpic/Rainer Droese; p. 28: © Christoph Mayer, Büro für Architektur und Städtebau, Berlin/photo Frank Hülsbömer, Berlin; pp. 33, 109, 110, 111, 112: © Sou Fujimoto Architects, Tokyo/photos Iwan Baan; p. 34: © Studio Liu Lubin; p. 37, 226: © June14 Meyer-Grohbrügge & Chermayeff, june-14.com; pp. 41, 48: © Herzog & de Meuron, Basel/private photos ; p. 42: © Bauwert Werderscher Markt GmbH, Berlin/Bad Kötzting; p. 52: © Hafencity/www.ueberseequartier.de; pp. 60, 81 (left), 152 (right): © photo Ivo Goetz, Berlin; p. 62: © Town & Country Haus Lizenzgeber GmbH, Hörselberg-Hainich/ private photo; pp. 66, 92, 102 (left), 187, 197, 204: © private photos; p. 71: © Photo Foster + Partners, Apple Inc. (left), © Gehry Architects. Courtesy of Gehry Partners/photo Everett Katigbak, Facebook (right); p. 74: © Hudson Yards Development Corporation/The City of New York/Kohn Pedersen Fox Associates, photo rendering by Visualhouse; p. 77: © Arch. Pierre Koenig/photo Julius Shulman, © The Getty Research Institute; p. 78: © akg-images/VIEW Pictures/photo Grant Smith; p. 81: © akg-images, photo Florian Profitlich (center), © picture alliance/dpa/photo Wolfgang Krumm (right); p. 83: © Daimler AG, Stuttgart; p. 88: © Shigeru Ban Architects, Paris Office (left), © Toyo Ito & Associates, Architects, Tokyo (right); p. 89: © Lacaton & Vassal Architects, Paris; p. 95: © private archive Claude Parent, Neuilly-sur-Seine; p. 98: © LEGO GmbH, Grasbrunn; p. 100: © Arch. Yoshiharu Tsukamoto, Atelier Bow-Wow, Tokyo/photo Iwan Baan; pp. 107, 135, 146: © SANAA/Ryue Nishizawa Architects, Tokyo/photos Iwan Baan; p. 128: © Stiftung Bauhaus Dessau (left, center), © Arch. Richard Kauffmann/photographer: unknown (right); p. 145: © SANAA/Ryue Nishizawa Architects, Tokyo, plan: SANAA; p. 148: © Office Yoshichika Takagi + Associates, Hokkaido (left, center), © Megumi Matsubara, Tokyo (right); pp. 150, 230: © Safdie Architects, Toronto (left), © Michael Maltzan Architecture, Inc., Los Angeles, CA (right); p. 152: © zanderroth architekten gmbh/photo: Simon Menges (left, center), © Baugemeinschaft R50, ifau + Jesko Fezer/Heide & von Beckerath, Berlin/photo Ivo Goetz, Berlin (right); p. 154: © Christian Brunner (top), © Martin Stollenwerk (bottom); p. 155: © carpaneto architekten, fatkoehl architekten, BARarchitekten, photo: DaKa; p. 159: © photo Wolfgang Stahr, Berlin; p. 177: © raumlabor Berlin; p. 180: © SANAA/Kazuyo Sejima + Ryue Nishizawa, Tokyo; p. 182: © John Bock, Berlin (top), © Tomás Saraceno, Berlin (bottom); p. 183: © Tobias Rehberger, Rehberger Studio, Frankfurt am Main (bottom); p. 188: © Zaha Hadid Architects, London (Design by Patrik Schumacher and Zaha Hadid) ; pp. 190, 191, 192: © Photos The Walt Disney Company; p. 194: © Riken Yamamoto & Fieldshop, Yokohama (left), © On Design Architects, 318 Santa Barbara, CA (right); p. 196: © Kazunari Sakamoto, Tokyo; p. 199: © Brandlhuber Architekten, Berlin; p. 200: © raumlabor Berlin, photo Rainer Schlautmann; p. 202: © Urban Think Tank; p. 206: © Christian Esteban Calle Figueroa; pp. 209, 210: © Moma PS1; p. 211: © shunya.net (top, center), 4ever.eu (bottom); pp. 213, 216: © photos Thomas Struth; p. 218: © Arch. Richard Meier/photographer: unknown (top)

Sources
p. 102 (center, right): Niklas Maak, "Vergangene Lust," *Süddeutsche Zeitung Magazin*, no. 49 (Munich: Magazin Verlagsgesellschaft Süddeutsche Zeitung, December 10, 1999); p. 117: Yoshio Futagawa (ed.), *Sou Fujimoto. Recent Project* (Tokyo: A.D.A. EDITA,

2013); p. 119: Pierre Pelot, *La vie des enfants. Au temps de la Préhistoire*, © 2006, Éditions de la Martinière, Paris; p. 123: Catherine Hall, "Trautes Heim," in *Geschichte des privaten Lebens*, vol. 4, ed. Philippe Ariès and Georges Duby (Frankfurt am Main, 1992); p. 124: Marylène Patou-Mathis, *La préhistoire*, from the *Voir L'Histoire* series (Paris: Fleurus Éditions, 2008); p. 127: Franziska Bollerey, *Architekturkonzeption der utopischen Sozialisten* (Munich: Heinz Moos, February 1986); p. 131: Jules Verne, *Les Cinq Cents Millions de la Bégum*, 1879, cover of the original French edition by the illustrator Léon Benett; p. 141: "Kollektivhuset I Stockholm," brochure from Staffan Lamm and Thomas Steinfeld, *Das Kollektivhaus. Utopie und Wirklichkeit eines Wohnexperiments* (Frankfurt am Main: S. Fischer, 2006); p. 144: www.the-share.jp.

Imprint

Project management
Karen Angne

Copyediting
Danko Szabó, Munich

Translation from the German
Bram Opstelten, Richmond, VA

Graphic design, typesetting, and production
Hannes Halder

Cover design
Ivo Goetz

Printing and binding by
Friedrich Pustet KG, Regensburg

Printed in Germany

For the work by Le Corbusier (p. 179): © FLC/VG Bild-Kunst, Bonn, 2015
For the works by Anish Kapoor (p. 189), Constant Anton Nieuwenhuys (p. 183),
Frank Lloyd Wright (p. 218): © VG Bild-Kunst, Bonn, 2015

© 2015 Hirmer Verlag GmbH, Munich, and the author

For the original German edition "Niklas Maak, Wohnkomplex":
© 2014 Carl Hanser Verlag, Munich

Bibliographic information published by the Deutsche Nationalbibliothek: The Deutsche Nationalbibliothek lists this publication in the Deutsche Nationalbibliografie; detailed bibliographic data is available on the Internet at http://www.dnb.de.

ISBN 978-3-7774-2410-1

www.hirmerpublishers.com